THE MINDFUL WORKFORCE PORTFOLIO

THE MINDFUL WORKER

LEARNING AND WORKING INTO THE 21ST CENTURY

Curtis Miles

Piedmont Technical College
Greenwood, South Carolina

H&H Publishing Company
Clearwater, Florida

H&H Publishing Company, Inc.

1231 Kapp Drive
Clearwater, FL 33765
(727) 442-7760
(800) 366-4079
FAX (727) 442-2195

THE MINDFUL WORKER

By Curtis Miles

Editing, Production
Karen Hackworth

Editorial Assistant
Priscilla Trimmier

Production Supervision
Robert D. Hackworth

Business Operations
Mike Ealy, Sally Marston

ISBN 0-943202-46-9

Library of Congress Catalog Number 94-078037

Printing is the lowest number: 10 9 8 7 6 5 4 3 2

Introduction to The Mindful Worker

"May you live in interesting times." This Chinese wish has blossomed in the United States in this last decade of the twentieth century. Our times are very interesting: exciting jobs beside expanding under-employment, information highways beside homelessness, religious faith beside radiation dumps, volunteer giving beside massive corruption, genetic wonders beside AIDS, drive-through restaurants beside drive-by violence, and so forth.

Such times tend to bring out the best in people and institutions. They also highlight our weaknesses. Aspects of ourselves and our institutions which can get by in more peaceful times cannot do so in interesting times. In peaceful times other parts of our group or our society can compensate for our weaknesses, and we can do the same for their's. Throwing money at problems, producing so much that significant amounts can be wasted, overlooking destructive behavior, or hiding inefficiency or wrong directions behind large staffs can overcome (or at least muffle) deep problems only when we can afford such practices.

Clearly, the United States in this decade no longer has the luxury of such excesses and blind spots. As but one example, parents, social institutions, and particularly employers no longer have the time, energy, or will to cover up the flaws in our educational systems. And teachers and schools, in their turn, are too stretched and stressed to compensate for all of the negative things that are influencing their students outside of the classroom. "Business as usual" no longer works for either party.

The Mindful Worker grew out of one such conflict of weaknesses: that between the workforce abilities which increasing number of employers must have in order to thrive and the very different abilities which our educational systems emphasize.

Employers – whether private corporations or public agencies – are being forced to change their ways in order to compete in the private sector and to remain accountable in the public sector. They don't want to change so dramatically (no one does), but they have little choice when faced with business competition or taxpayer anger. How are they changing? Downsizing, reorganizing, cutting budgets, modifying customer-supplier relationships, replacing short-term profits with notions of quality, measuring their effectiveness: many different ways for many different organizations.

One consistent thread across all of these responses, however, is a pervasive impact on the individual worker. Educational credentials, by themselves, no longer guarantee job satisfaction and security, although the *lack* of credentials is increasingly a guarantee of no security and satisfaction. Increasing numbers of people are having to settle for part-time or temporary jobs. Layoffs are accelerating. People are being asked to do more.

Beneath such widely-reported dilemmas lies a much more significant shift in the workforce. Employers are placing much more of a premium on workers with **broad work and personal competencies**. Effective managerial and organizational responses to "interesting times" place much greater responsibility on the workforce. This often implies responsibility not so much for greater productions as for greater flexibility and participation in making the company or agency successful. Specialized technical knowledge and skill are prized and always will be. But increasingly employers seek employees who have broad competencies in such areas as problem solving, teamwork, communications, managing goals, leadership, learning, dependability, and systems thinking.

Increasingly, job satisfaction and security will come mainly to those with such competencies. "Interesting times," in this case, demands and rewards people who can keep adjusting to change, who can be self-starting contributors to organizations which need their leadership and flexibility, and above all who can keep learning as these interesting times bring about continual change. It doesn't matter if the person is the company attorney, a top manager, or a line worker – all need to "be in charge" of their area of expertise and responsibility.

Which brings us to the other half of the equation: the educational system, and particularly the higher education systems. By and large, colleges and universities emphasize specialized disciplines: study of a particular subject such as chemistry, accounting, literature, or philosophy. Even the "general education core" resembles a disciplinary specialty writ small: introduction to psychology, philosophy, history, etc.

Such an emphasis has great value. But it also has weaknesses, and one of them is in the very area which American employers now need the most. Few college students ever encounter, much less master, those generalized competencies in any systematic way. Higher education's dynamics simply do not emphasize broad, generalized competencies such as responsibility, leadership, teamwork, non-technical problem solving, and the like. No educational system can do everything, and this is one of the things which ours does not do well. There are few, if any, courses in these areas, and no focused texts which might serve as a guide for such courses.

Thus *The Mindful Worker*. This is an attempt to at least skim the surface of seventeen generalized competencies which will probably make a major difference in your job success and satisfaction in the 21st century, no matter what job you hold. It helps you explore – hopefully in a lively and personally meaningful way – what those competencies are, how they work, and what they mean in the workplace. It helps you analyze your strengths and weaknesses with each competency, and guides you in laying out a plan for your own personal development in each area – to be pursued as you choose. The hope is that, as you take this exploration to heart, you and others like you will begin to mend the weakness in the connection between education and employment which our "interesting times" will no longer allow us to tolerate.

No book is created in a vacuum; books require a nurturing environment. *The Mindful Worker's* nurturers are fourfold. First are those who have poured out tolerance, support, and love during my endless computer and research hours: my family. Deepest of thanks, appreciation, and returned love to my wife Barbara and our children, Kendall, Diana, and Stuart. The second nurturer is an extraordinary friend, questioner, encourager, thinker, publisher, and general agent of interesting times: Bob Hackworth, owner of

H&H Publishing and consort of Gladys, a very special lady. The third is an exceptional editor and friend, Karen Davis.

Beyond the personal nurturers, however, lies a more general group. They are that variety of people who have helped me (sort of) understand and (greatly) believe in the reality and power of what is now occurring in American workplaces and American society. Some I have talked with, worked with, learned from, and observed. Many, as diverse as J. Edwards Deming, Anthony Carnevale, and Harold Hodgkinson, I have just read and heard.

With such nurturers, actually writing *The Mindful Worker* became an inevitable event as well as a leap of faith. Faith that colleges will find ways to break free from their disciplinary orientation long enough to find or create courses in which guides like this may encounter students. And faith that the students, having encountered such guides, will remove their entrenched "student mindsets" long enough to take what they discover to heart, as having direct and important personal meaning for them.

Curtis Miles
August, 1994

THE MINDFUL WORKER TABLE OF CONTENTS

1   KEY COMPETENCIES FOR SUCCESS IN THE 21ST CENTURY   1

    A.   What Does it Take to Succeed at a Job?   3
    B.   Working Into The Twenty-first Century   9
    C.   Another View of the 21st Century Workplace   15
    D.   Assessing Your Preparedness for Becoming a Mindful Worker   18
    E.   The Mindful Worker   23
    Summary of Chapter 1   25
    Chapter 1 Review Questions   26

2   IT ONLY HURTS WHEN I THINK ABOUT IT!   27

    A.   What's the Problem with Problems?   29
    B.   What Kind of Problem is That, Anyway?   31
    C.   Comparing Two Problem-Solving Strategies   36
    D.   Solution-Oriented Problem Solving   39
    E.   Stage 1 – Clarify the Problem   41
    F.   Stage 2 – Identify Alternative Solutions   45
    G.   Stage 3 – Analyze Alternative Solutions   48
    H.   Stages 4 & 5 – Selecting and Checking the Solution   51
    I.   Putting the Pieces Together Again   54
    J.   Roadblocks on the Way to Problem-Solving   58
    K.   Problem-Solving: Making Your Map   59
    Summary of Chapter 2   61
    Chapter 2 Review Questions   62

3   EVERYBODY'S GOT A SYSTEM   63

    A.   Interdependence: We're All In It Together   65
    B.   Systems Thinking: Applied Interdependence   70
    C.   Cause-Oriented Problem Solving   76
    D.   Stage 1b: Identify Alternative Causes   78
    E.   Stage 1c: Analyze Possible Causes   84
    F.   The Seven Stages of Cause-Oriented Problem Solving   91
    G.   Systems: Making Your Map   94
    Summary of Chapter 3   97
    Chapter 3 Review Questions   98

4   WHO'S IN CHARGE HERE ANYWAY?   99

    Taking Your Mind Off Of Autopilot: An Introduction   101
    A.   Metacognition: Getting In Touch With Our Minds   102
    B.   Goals: Managing Where You're Going and How to Get There   108

C. Time: Managing One of Your Most Important Resources   113
D. Stress: Controlling the Cannibal of Your Performance   117
E. Taking Charge: Making Your Map   122
Summary of Chapter 4   126
Chapter 4 Review Questions   127

5 WHO ARE THESE PEOPLE AND WHAT DO THEY WANT?   129

A. Working With Others, Individually   131
B. Teams: What's It All About?   136
C. Teams: How Do They Do That?   141
D. Lead, Follow, or Get Out of the Way   146
E. Leadership: How Do They Do That?   151
F. Leadership in a Team-based Environment   157
G. Other People: Making Your Map   158
Summary of Chapter 5   161
Chapter 5 Review Questions   162

6 TELL ME AGAIN WHO YOU ARE?   163

Introduction to Chapter 6   165
A. "Can Adapt To Change" – Flexibility   166
B. "Can Be Counted On" – Dependability   171
C. "Will Shoulder The Burden" – Taking Responsibility   175
D. "Can Be Trusted" – Honesty   180
E. "Really Wants To Perform" – Motivation   185
F. Key Personal Traits: Making Your Map   191
Summary of Chapter 6   196
Chapter 6 Review Questions   197

7 IT'S ALL IN YOUR MIND – SOMEWHERE!   199

A. Learning Into the Twenty-first Century   201
B. Beyond Mrs. Hackaberry: Learning about Learning   204
C. Information Processing: The 'How' of Learning   207
D. Input: The First Stage of Learning   212
E. Processing: The Critical Stage in Learning   215
F. Output: The Payoff in Learning   221
G. When the System Breaks Down: Forgetting   224
H. Why is that Medicine Good for Me?   226
I. Learning on the Job   228
J. Updating the Flow of Information Processing   230
K. Learning: Making Your Map   231
Summary of Chapter 7   232
Chapter 7 Review Questions   233

8 IMPROVING YOURSELF AS A MINDFUL WORKER   235

CHAPTER 1

KEY COMPETENCIES
FOR SUCCESS IN
THE 21ST CENTURY

Exercise 1A
WHAT DOES IT TAKE TO SUCCEED AT A JOB?

Working is working, right? You spend time and energy and you get money. If you spend more time and energy, you get more money. This viewpoint suggests that 'time and energy' are the main things that determine your job success. Does this fit with your experience? Does a lawyer make so much more than a fast-food cook only because he or she works longer and harder? Or are there some other factors to consider?

Let's ask the question another way. Do local singers and band leaders make less money than international rock stars simply because they don't work as hard or as long? Does one student get A's while another gets C's just because the first one studies longer and harder? Or are there other explanations for success?

Obviously, more than 'time and energy' is needed for job success. There are other factors to consider—things like motivation, self-discipline, level of skill, and luck. These are some of the very important 'success factors' which help determine your success on the job.

But that leads to another question. Do these success factors work with every job? Are they the same for a lawyer, a fast-food cook, an entertainer, and a student? In other words, if we could find out what these factors were, and if we could become skilled at them, then would we be very likely to succeed in *any* sort of job?

There's no certain answer to that question, but it's the one we will *begin* to answer in this exercise. As we begin, write out below the important questions that this introduction has raised for you.

✍ **QUESTIONS TO THINK ABOUT**

This exercise is designed to help you think about things that you already know something about – but perhaps in a different way.

First, pick an occupation you wish to analyze. Pick a type of job you know something about. Or you might choose one of these: nurse, police officer, welfare case worker, physical therapist, office manager, auto mechanic, counselor, assembly line worker, secretary, salesperson, accountant.

Second, decide what competencies someone needs to succeed in that occupation. "Competency" means having a suitable amount of a particular skill. Think about the occupation you've chosen. Then ask yourself what skills or behaviors someone needs for success in that particular occupation. List them in the box below.

Don't worry about very technical skills; look for general competencies. *For example*, if you were listing the success competencies of a teacher you might mention general things like: good speaker, organized, motivated, a good learner. Look for charateristics that could describe people in many different kinds of jobs.

✍ **WHAT ARE SOME SUCCESS COMPETENCIES FOR A** _____ ?

◊

◊

◊

◊

◊

◊

◊

As a class you've now listed some success competencies of several different occupations. What do they have (mostly) in common? Compare your lists, then list any competencies you find that are important to most of those occupations you have listed. You may need to re-word or expand some of them.

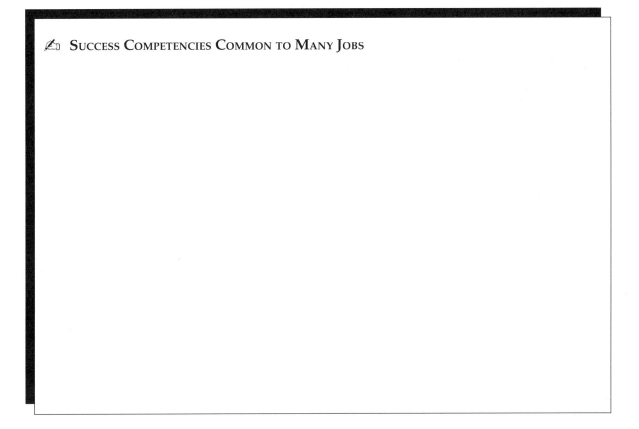

✎ SUCCESS COMPETENCIES COMMON TO MANY JOBS

Finally, discuss the following three questions:

◊ Is it likely that the competencies you have listed above are important in *all* or almost all occupations?

◊ Can you think of occupations where one or another of those competencies is not very important? What occupations? Why are they not very important?

◊ Why do you suppose that these competencies are important to success in so many occupations? See if you can get 'below the surface' of this question.

This book is about your success in the changing, confusing world of the 21st century. "Success" is a slippery term. Is someone who spends almost every hour working, and becomes very wealthy and famous, a successful person? Perhaps. Is someone who spends the minimum time at work, and devotes great time to a hobby, a successful person? Perhaps. How about someone who makes little, never marries, yet contributes greatly to government, the arts, charities, etc.? Perhaps. How about someone who concentrates on her/his family? Perhaps.

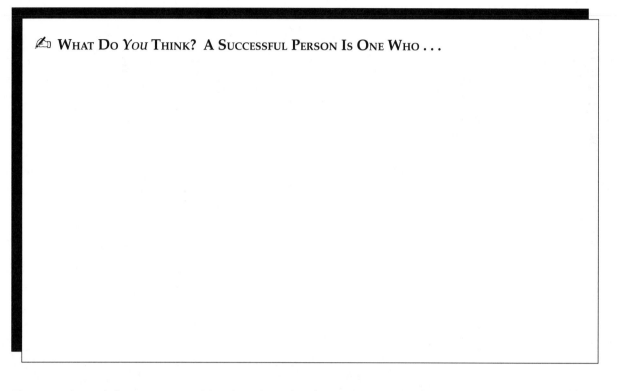

✍ **What Do *You* Think? A Successful Person Is One Who . . .**

The next part of this exercise tackles this idea of success. We are going to build on what you did earlier. You created a list of occupational success competencies. Let's see how important those competencies might be for *other* roles we play in life: as parent, spouse, student, etc.

The matrix on the opposite page is designed to compare your job success competencies with other important life roles. Look at it, and then read the following instructions.

◊   Across the top are several columns for different roles we play in life. There are two empty columns in case you want to explore other life roles. The heading says, "If you want to be good at this role . . ." Notice that the emphasis is not just on *doing* that role, but on *being good* at that role.

◊   Down the left side are blank rows, waiting for the success competencies you identified earlier. Notice the heading across the side, which says: "Does it help to be good at this . . . ?"

Complete the matrix, following these instructions:

STEP 1.   Fill in the rows on the left side with the common success competencies you identified two pages ago.

STEP 2.   Fill in the first vertical column (parent) by rating how important each competency is for being a successful parent. Use this scale:

V = Very important   I = Important   L = Limited Importance

(If it's not important, leave the box blank)

STEP 3.   Then complete the ratings for the other life roles.

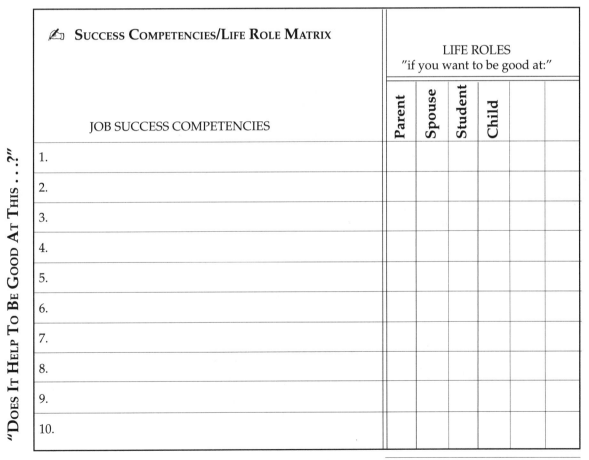

✍ Now Explore The Information You Find In The Completed Matrix.

◊   List the job success competencies which seem to be important in
    all or most of these life roles.

◊   Which of these life roles depend for success on the largest number
    of job success competencies?

◊   Do the life roles you listed just above seem a lot like 'working'?

◊   Are there any other success competencies that are very important in
    these other life roles, but aren't crucial on the job?

◊   If you're good with a competency in one role (e.g. on the job) will
    you be good at it in another role (e.g. as a spouse)? Why/why not?

Exercise 1B
WORKING INTO THE TWENTY-FIRST CENTURY

"Change is eternal," says the philosopher. Yet there are times when things change very slowly, and other times when they change strongly and seemingly as fast as lightning. We are in one of the world's lightning periods.

Don't believe it? Consider what have emerged as every-day realities in the past decade or so. Portable computers, cellular telephones, FAX machines, MTV, video recorders, the drug epidemic, AIDS, the collapse of the cold war, and on and on. See how many other significant things you can think of which have emerged in your lifetime.

Below is a chart comparing a more subtle, but more powerful, area of change: change in the characteristics of the workplace. Today most companies are somewhere between the traditional and the 'high performance' model of the workplace. But within a decade most will be well over to the right side.

Read, compare, think about, and discuss the elements of these models, and what the 'high performance' model implies for the types of workers needed.

CHARACTERISTICS OF TODAY'S AND TOMORROW'S WORKPLACE

TRADITIONAL MODEL	HIGH PERFORMANCE MODEL
STRATEGY	
◊ mass production	◊ flexible production
◊ long production runs	◊ customized production runs
◊ centralized control	◊ decentralized control
PRODUCTION	
◊ fixed automation	◊ flexible automation
◊ end-of-line quality control	◊ on-line quality control
◊ fragmentation of tasks	◊ multi-skilled worker teams
◊ authority of supervisor	◊ authority delegated to worker
HUMAN RESOURCES	
◊ labor-management confrontation	◊ labor-management cooperation
◊ minimal qualifications accepted	◊ basic skills abilities required
◊ workers as a cost, throw-away	◊ workers as an investment
JOB LADDERS	
◊ internal promotion	◊ limited internal promotion
◊ advancement by seniority	◊ advancement by certified skills
TRAINING	
◊ minimal for production workers	◊ training sessions for everyone
◊ specialized for craft workers	◊ broader skills sought

SOURCE: 'Competing in the New International Economy.' Washington, DC: Office of Technology Assessment, 1990.

Some of the items on that list may not be very familiar to you. Let's go over them briefly. But at the same time let's reflect on what those changes in production models mean for a typical industrial worker. What is happening with production workers is also happening with most other occupations, though in different degrees. Below is a list of success competencies which probably includes most of the ones you created in the last exercise. As we discuss each of the five aspects of the models, **list which of the competencies are increasingly important with the high performance workplace model**.

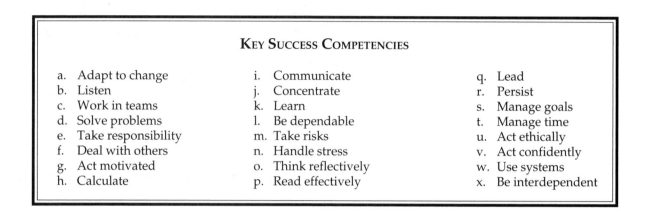

KEY SUCCESS COMPETENCIES

a. Adapt to change
b. Listen
c. Work in teams
d. Solve problems
e. Take responsibility
f. Deal with others
g. Act motivated
h. Calculate

i. Communicate
j. Concentrate
k. Learn
l. Be dependable
m. Take risks
n. Handle stress
o. Think reflectively
p. Read effectively

q. Lead
r. Persist
s. Manage goals
t. Manage time
u. Act ethically
v. Act confidently
w. Use systems
x. Be interdependent

MANUFACTURING STRATEGY

The traditional industrial model calls for long mass-production runs under centralized control. What does that mean? Many, most, or all of the separate production lines in the plant would run the same product day-in-and-day-out for days, weeks, or even months. Decisions and management of this production would all come 'from the top.' Everyone else would just carry out the orders.

Under the high performance model, however, many or all of the separate production lines may be running totally or partly different products. A line might make a given product for only hours or days: a custom order for a particular customer. Decisions and management of these varied processes lie much more with the 'line troops': operators, engineers, supervisors, and so forth.

✐ Look at the listed success competencies. Which are increasingly important for high-performance manufacturing?

PRODUCTION DYNAMICS

In a traditional model, both people and machines were set to do one specialized job, endlessly. Supervisors gave the orders and did the thinking. Products were inspected for defects only at the end of the line, and defective items were then scrapped, sent back for re-work, or sold at reduced prices.

In the high performance model, both people and machines can do a variety of jobs and the 'line' workers have much more decision-making and authority, often while working in teams. Quality is inspected and tracked throughout production, to catch and cure problems when they first emerge.

✍ Look at the listed success competencies. Which are increasingly important for quality production dynamics?

HUMAN RESOURCES

How do attitudes and treatment of people compare in the two philosophies? In the traditional model people were 'hands' – hired to do a job requiring more physical motion than anything else, with limited need for intellect since the jobs were specialized and repetitive. If a process could be done with three rather than four machines, fine: fewer hands were needed. Management and labor unions thus tended to be adversaries: suspicious, uncooperative, protective of their own turf.

The high performance model hires people at least partly as 'heads' in addition to hands. Basic mental and physical skills are important, since decision-making and authority are pushed down much closer to the line with the new production methods. Workers are an investment; experience and skill is valued and developed. Management and labor unions tend to work more closely together, realizing a common stake in the success of the plant.

✍ Look at the listed success competencies. Which are increasingly important within this view of human resources?

Job Ladders

Consider the implications of long-run mass production, specialization, and treatment of workers as 'hands.' What was needed for promotion? Experience and 'time-in-grade,' plus proof by action that one was reliable. Special knowledge and skills were not vital, and outsiders were unknown quantities. Unions fought hard to protect the rights of their own members. Thus the traditional model was one of hiring from within and advancement by seniority.

These dynamics change with the high performance model. Positions are often "advertised" first within the company, but experience and time-in-grade are insufficient for promotion. Learning, development, and certification are required. With movement of authority/responsibility farther down the line, traits like leadership, teamwork, and expertise become more important, and "reliability" is less crucial. Thus more hiring comes from outside.

✍ Look at the listed success competencies. Which are increasingly important with this type of career ladder?

Training

Continued education and training also have different dynamics in the two models. Under the traditional model, 'hands' needed little additional skill, while specialized technical workers did require periodic upgrading. But learning was not a major focus of employer or employee concern.

Within the high performance model, training is continuous for almost every worker. Why? Because everyone has greater involvement in decisions, in changes in production and management, and in general company success. Both continual training and – in particular – the broad abilities that support employee ability to grow and change are valued.

✍ Look at the listed success competencies. Which are increasingly important with this emphasis on training?

The differences between the traditional and high-performance models of production are only one factor to consider in preparing for the 21st century. Consider also the nature of various jobs – and in particular the things you like and dislike. All jobs aren't the same, even within the same occupation. Stop and think for a minute about what that means. Let's take the occupation of 'writer' as an example. Consider the many different ways in which you might write for a living:

◊   Newspaper reporter, rushing about and working in a chaotic news room.
◊   Advertising writer, working with a small group of professionals.
◊   Textbook or novel writer, working alone in front of a computer.
◊   Report writer, taking information from others and tying words around it.

The dynamics are very different among these jobs, even though they are in the same occupation. What dynamics do you prefer in a job? This exercise will help you clarify your values.

The chart below has 11 opposite pairs of traits: for example, working alone vs working with others. Place a checkmark in one of the boxes separating each pair, to show which one you prefer (and how strongly).

	Very Important	Somewhat Important	Not Important	Somewhat Important	Very Important	
Work alone	_____	_____	_____	_____	_____	Work with others
No/little supervision	_____	_____	_____	_____	_____	Close supervision
Very competitive	_____	_____	_____	_____	_____	Not competitive
Little responsibility	_____	_____	_____	_____	_____	Much responsibility
"Close is good enough" standards	_____	_____	_____	_____	_____	Very exact standards
The same daily tasks	_____	_____	_____	_____	_____	Varied daily tasks
Physically active	_____	_____	_____	_____	_____	Passive work
Slow-paced	_____	_____	_____	_____	_____	Fast-paced
A lot of structure	_____	_____	_____	_____	_____	Little structure
Risky/challenging	_____	_____	_____	_____	_____	Safe/secure
Short-term results	_____	_____	_____	_____	_____	Long-term results

Let's try to identify a few job situations that might fit your values. Your ratings may give you some sense of the kind of job and job setting which you would value. Alone, or with a partner, jot down below at least two specific job situations that would seem to fit your values.

✍ **JOB SITUATIONS THAT WOULD FIT MY VALUES**

Do the job situations like the ones above 'ring true' for you? Are they the kinds of environments that you think you'd like? If so, are they in your career 'game plan' in terms of what you are preparing for and looking for? If not, you might have some important thinking to do.

Now let's look at the degree of match between your preferred environment and your school environment.

For this task, **circle the side of each pair on the previous page which is most like an academic school setting**. For example, in most schools we work alone more than with others, so you would circle that side. If you think both sides apply equally, leave the pair blank.

Your circles, compared with your checkmarks, suggests how closely the academic classroom environment matches your preferred environment. To analyze what that might mean, answer the questions in the next column.

QUESTION 1
In which areas is your preference least like academic classrooms?

QUESTION 2
Do you think that a mis-match (if there is one) has an impact on your performance in school? If so, how?

QUESTION 3
Do you think that a mis-match (if there is one) will have an impact on your later performance in the workplace? If so, how?

QUESTION 4
What might you do to minimize the impact on any mismatches you have?

Exercise 1C
ANOTHER VIEW OF THE 21ST CENTURY WORKPLACE

Much that you have explored up until this point in this book paints a picture of a certain type of worker in demand in the future. That picture is of the mindful worker: thoughtful, skilled at learning, reliable, a team player, a good communicator, and so forth. There will certainly be many jobs like that – and they will be the most satisfying for most of us.

Yet there is a darker cloud in this crystal ball: a murky picture of a different type of workforce, workplace, and employment opportunities. Consider these factors:

◊ Increasing proportions of the workforce are employed in the service industry, which in many cases means places like McDonald's, Wal-Mart, telemarketing, and the like. How well does your experience with these types of jobs fit with the image of the mindful worker?

◊ A growing trend in many companies is to hire part-time and temporary employees rather than full-time employees. Many of these workers get lower wages, have few if any benefits, and lack any form of job security. How does this fit with the notion (from the chart in the last exercise) of workers as an investment?

◊ "Downsizing"–meaning laying off many workers – is a reality in many American businesses. Some statistics: unemployment increased by 2.5 million people between July of 1990 and March of 1992; Fortune 500 companies (the 500 'biggest and best' American companies) laid off 480,000 employees in 1991; and from 1992 through 1997 the military will 'lay off' about 548,000 people. How does this fit with the idea of employers eagerly seeking new crops of mindful workers?

◊ Average earnings for non-agricultural workers in the United States have been steadily dropping since about 1970: an average weekly earning of $387.24 in 1969 dropped to $335.20 in 1989, and has dropped since then.

◊ The proportion of new high school graduates who are finding new full-time jobs has dropped very rapidly, and college graduates are finding greater difficulty in obtaining the level of job for which they are educationally qualified. High school dropouts are in very deep, and perhaps permanent, trouble in terms of finding meaningful employment.

◊ Over the past decade employee satisfaction is down for every major aspect of a job – salary, benefits, hours worked, colleagues, promotion opportunity, personal satisfaction, and the social importance of their work.

◊ Business spends about $30 billion annually on education and training, but over 70% of it goes to those who already have a college degree.

These are disturbing pieces of information. They don't seem to fit neatly with the idea of great employment opportunities open to those possessing the competencies of mindful workers. Spend some thoughtful time and energy – *right now* – wrestling with these inconsistencies.

✍ **Write a thoughtful, full-page answer to the question on the following page.**

✍ HOW CAN WE INTERPRET THE APPARENT INCONSISTENCIES BETWEEN THE DATA ON THE PREVIOUS PAGE AND THE IDEAS OF THE MINDFUL WORKER?

It's not easy to bring these two possible futures to-gether, is it? That's the trouble with predicting the future. At any given moment there is evidence to support several different possibilities. And, usually, what actually occurs is something a little different from any of them. If that makes you uneasy, good! Because the working world of the early 21st century will be an uneasy place, with rapid change more common than any of us might like. One of the skills of the mindful worker is the ability to tolerate (if not like) uneasiness and ambiguity.

There is, then, no 'right answer' as to how to bring these possible futures together. Your answers may well be as correct as anyone else's. However, there is at least one glimmer of a likely explanation. Examine the chart to the right carefully.

What does that chart seem to say? That in America in recent years the rich got richer and the poor got poorer. And the middle class started disappearing. Notice the top horizontal line. It suggests that 30% of American citizens had more than their share of American income (54% of it) in 1967. And that, twenty years later, they had an even higher percentage (58%). By now, that 30% of our population probably has 60% of the American income. Meanwhile, the other 70% of Americans have a part of America's wealth that is steadily shrinking.

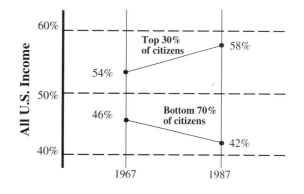

Distribution of income in the
U.S. between 1967 and 1987

Income, of course, is not the only standard by which we can judge 'success,' 'happiness,' and the other things we hope for. There are growing numbers who argue that the *most* fundamental change which will occur during the next decade or two will be in re-defining 'success' to place less emphasis on income and more emphasis on other aspects of life.

Yet no matter what the likelihood of that change, income will clearly have some significant impact on our lives. In that context, as we close this exercise, examine the above chart while you answer the fol-lowing questions.

✍ **HOW MANY OF THOSE IN THE 'TOP 30%' WILL BE MINDFUL WORKERS?**

IF THERE *IS* A MIDDLE CLASS, HOW MANY OF *THEM* WILL BE MINDFUL WORKERS?

Exercise 1D
ASSESSING YOUR PREPAREDNESS FOR BECOMING A MINDFUL WORKER

Clearly, no matter how employment patterns work out, the mindful workers will have a much better chance of ending up in a satisfying position. How well are you equipped with the competencies needed by the mindful worker in the 21st century? And how important *are* those other competencies, anyway? This exercise helps you begin exploring those two questions.

Following is a list of 24 job success competencies associated with the mindful worker: the list you encountered earlier. You have three tasks in this exercise: to decide *which* competencies are more important, to decide *why* each one is important, and to rate your preparedness with each of them.

a.	Adapt to change	i.	Communicate	q.	Lead
b.	Listen	j.	Concentrate	r.	Persist
c.	Work in teams	k.	Learn	s.	Manage goals
d.	Solve problems	l.	Be dependable	t.	Manage time
e.	Take responsibility	m.	Take risks	u.	Act ethically
f.	Deal with others	n.	Handle stress	v.	Act confidently
g.	Act motivated	o.	Think reflectively	w.	Use systems
h.	Calculate	p.	Read effectively	x.	Be interdependent

STEP 1: Judge the relative importance of each competency. Think about how they have been described, and what you know about the mindful worker in the 21st century. Then prioritize these compentencies in the boxes below in terms of their relative importance

✍ THE TOP EIGHT COMPETENCIES ARE:

✍ THE MIDDLE EIGHT COMPETENCIES ARE:

STEP 2: Clarify the significance of each of these competencies. Divide those competencies among the class members. Each person should give a one sentence explanation of why that competency is important to the mindful worker. Jot down what others say about those competencies in the following lists.

✍ **THIS COMPETENCY IS IMPORTANT TO THE MINDFUL WORKER BECAUSE . . .**

    a.   ADAPTING TO CHANGE:

    b.   LISTENING:

    c.   WORKING IN TEAMS:

    d.   SOLVING PROBLEMS:

    e.   TAKING RESPONSIBILITY:

    f.   DEALING WITH OTHERS:

    g.   ACTING MOTIVATED:

    h.   CALCULATING:

    i.   COMMUNICATING:

✍ **This Competency Is Important To The Mindful Worker Because . . .**

j.   CONCENTRATING:

k.   LEARNING:

l.   BEING DEPENDABLE:

m.   TAKING RISKS:

n.   HANDLING STRESS:

o.   THINKING REFLECTIVELY:

p.   READING EFFECTIVELY:

q.   LEADING:

r.   PERSISTING:

s.   MANAGING GOALS:

t.   MANAGING TIME:

u.   ACTING ETHICALLY:

v.   ACTING CONFIDENTLY:

w.   USING SYSTEMS:

x.   BEING INTERDEPENDENT:

How do your ratings compare with the experts? Well, the experts all talk about the same sorts of competencies, but there's no one master list that they all agree upon. Here, however, is how those competencies fared in seven major studies of mindful worker's competencies: how many of the studies listed them.

MINDFUL WORKER COMPETENCIES CITED IN SEVEN MAJOR STUDIES		
Listed in all 7	Listed in 6 of 7	Listed in 2-5 of 7
Adapt to change.	Take responsibility.	Listen.
Work in teams.	Act motivated.	Concentrate.
Solve problems.	Read effectively.	Be dependable.
Deal with others.	Lead.	Take risks.
Calculate.	Manage goals.	Manage stress.
Communicate.	Act confidently.	Think reflectively.
Learn.	Use systems.	Persist.
		Manage time.
		Act ethically.
		Be interdependent.

Compare your conclusions with their expert judgments. If you were close, congratulations! If you weren't, don't worry about it; we're *all* guessing!

STEP 3: The final task in this exercise is perhaps the most important: to make your own judgment as to how you stack up with each of these competencies. You've discussed each of them. You've compared their importance. You've seen how business people compare their importance. Now compare yourself against them, as candidly as possible.

Complete the ratings below. As you decide how to rate yourself, think of situations in which you have been called on to exhibit that behavior. For example, taking responsibility for solving a sudden group problem, or listening actively in class. How did you perform? Rate yourself.

✍ **How Prepared Are You To Do This Consistently?**

		TOTALLY	MOSTLY	SOME-TIMES	SELDOM	ALMOST NEVER	NOT SURE
◊	ADAPT TO CHANGE?	_____	_____	_____	_____	_____	_____
◊	LISTEN?	_____	_____	_____	_____	_____	_____
◊	WORK IN TEAMS?	_____	_____	_____	_____	_____	_____
◊	SOLVE PROBLEMS?	_____	_____	_____	_____	_____	_____
◊	TAKE RESPONSIBILITY?	_____	_____	_____	_____	_____	_____
◊	DEAL WITH OTHERS?	_____	_____	_____	_____	_____	_____
◊	ACT MOTIVATED?	_____	_____	_____	_____	_____	_____
◊	CALCULATE?	_____	_____	_____	_____	_____	_____
◊	COMMUNICATE?	_____	_____	_____	_____	_____	_____
◊	CONCENTRATE?	_____	_____	_____	_____	_____	_____
◊	LEARN?	_____	_____	_____	_____	_____	_____
◊	BE DEPENDABLE?	_____	_____	_____	_____	_____	_____
◊	TAKE RISKS?	_____	_____	_____	_____	_____	_____
◊	HANDLE STRESS?	_____	_____	_____	_____	_____	_____
◊	THINK REFLECTIVELY?	_____	_____	_____	_____	_____	_____
◊	READ EFFECTIVELY?	_____	_____	_____	_____	_____	_____
◊	LEAD?	_____	_____	_____	_____	_____	_____
◊	PERSIST?	_____	_____	_____	_____	_____	_____
◊	MANAGE GOALS?	_____	_____	_____	_____	_____	_____
◊	MANAGE TIME?	_____	_____	_____	_____	_____	_____
◊	ACT ETHICALLY?	_____	_____	_____	_____	_____	_____
◊	ACT CONFIDENTLY?	_____	_____	_____	_____	_____	_____
◊	USE SYSTEMS?	_____	_____	_____	_____	_____	_____
◊	BE INTERDEPENDENT?	_____	_____	_____	_____	_____	_____

How did you come out? Again, bear in mind that this is a *self* rating. Some of you may have rated yourself too highly, which you might want to be careful about when interpreting the results. A number of you probably rated yourself too low on some competencies; you've probably got more going for you than you think. Keep remembering: we can *all* improve on *each* of these competencies.

Exercise 1E
THE MINDFUL WORKER

The following quote from an important study entitled <u>Workplace Basics</u> captures the idea of the mindful worker. Those alert private or public companies who are shifting to meet the new economic world before it runs them down do not just *want* this kind of worker. They *must have* this kind of worker if they are going to compete successfully. If they don't compete successfully, of course, then they won't need any workers at all – and another business will close . . .

*"Many employers say that the most important skills for any employee are the academic triumvirate - reading, writing, and computation. With increasing regularity, employers are telling the media, 'Give me people who can read, write, and do simple math and I'll train them for the jobs I have available.' But probing further, one finds that employers want good basic academic skills **and much more**.*

Employer complaints (about the preparedness of new workers) focus on serious deficiencies in areas that include problem-solving, personal management, and interpersonal skills. The abilities to conceptualize, organize, and verbalize thoughts, resolve conflicts, and work in teams are increasingly cited as critical.

Their concern is driven by the most compelling of circumstances - economic need. Competitive challenges are forcing employers to adopt an array of competitive strategies that can only be successfully implemented by an innovative and flexible workforce.

Beneath the surface comments about basic skills deficiencies lie employer concerns that they will not be able to achieve their competitive goals with their existing workforce. That they will not be able to successfully integrate new technology or sophisticated production processes. That basic workforce skills deficiencies are beginning to affect their bottom line.

So what are the skills - these basic workplace skills - that employers want? They certainly include basic skills associated with formal schooling. But academic skills such as reading, writing, and arithmetic comprise just the tip of the iceberg.

Employers want employees who can learn the particular skills of an available job - who have 'learned how to learn.' Employers want employees who will hear the key points that make up a customer's concerns and who can convey an adequate response.

Employers want employees who can think on their feet and who can come up with innovative solutions when needed. Employers want employees who have pride in themselves and their potential to be successful; who know how to get things done; and who have some sense of the skills needed to perform well in the workplace.

Employers want employees who can get along with customers, suppliers, and co-workers; who can work with others to achieve a goal; who have some sense of where the organization is headed and what they must do to make a contribution; and who can assume responsibility and motivate co-workers when necessary.

This is a prescription for a well-rounded worker who has acquired a number of discrete skills and who has the capability to acquire more sophisticated skills when necessary."

Think about the kind of worker that this government report suggests is needed, then answer the following questions.

✍ **HOW MUCH DO I WANT THAT KIND OF WORK?**

WHAT CAN I DO IN SCHOOL TO STRENGTHEN THOSE SORTS OF SKILLS?

HOW CAN I PROVE TO AN EMPLOYER THAT I HAVE THOSE SORTS OF SKILLS?

HOW MUCH MORE WILL THE NEEDED COMPETENCIES CHANGE IN THE NEXT TEN YEARS?

Summary of Chapter 1
KEY COMPETENCIES FOR SUCCESS IN THE 21ST CENTURY

As you have probably guessed, this book is more a personal journey than a text to read, memorize, and forget. What you are exploring might pay off very heavily for you in the future, depending on how seriously you take it. In learning, it helps *a lot* to summarize what you've been reading, thinking, and doing.

Therefore each chapter will end with a summary page. An invitation for you to think about, distill, and write down the key things you got from that chapter. They are whatever is important *to you*: information, ideas, or your own insights.

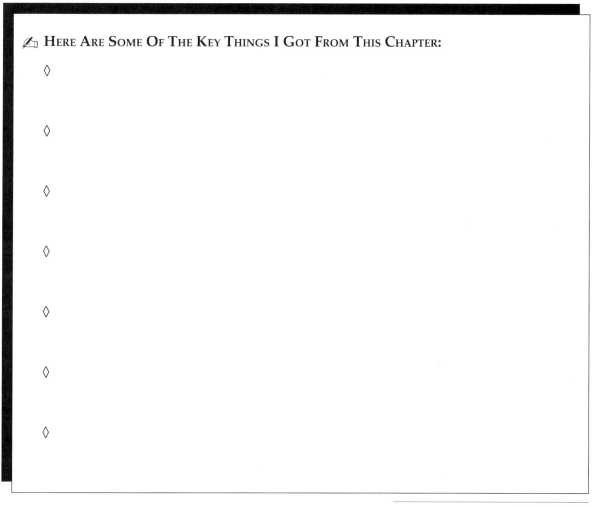

✍ HERE ARE SOME OF THE KEY THINGS I GOT FROM THIS CHAPTER:

◊

◊

◊

◊

◊

◊

◊

CHAPTER 1 – REVIEW QUESTIONS

1. If you are good with a particular success competency on the job, will you also be good with it in other life roles (parent, spouse, etc.)? Explain why or why not.

2. Compare the characteristics of the traditional model and the high performance model of the workplace in terms of how they operate and what this requires of the worker.

3. Identify five success competencies which are particularly important in a high-performance workplace. Explain *why* each one is particularly important in that type of workplace.

4. This chapter has presented two different visions of working in the 21st century. Compare and contrast those two visions: what they are, why both are likely, and what it means in terms of workforce satisfaction and competencies.

5. Explain the meaning and personal implications of the chart on page 17.

CHAPTER 2

IT ONLY HURTS WHEN I THINK ABOUT IT

MINDFUL WORKER COMPETENCIES
EXPLORED IN CHAPTER 2

Chapter 1 identified some two dozen competencies which are important in the high performance workplace. Chapters 2 through 7 explore seventeen of those competencies of the mindful worker. Examining so many different competencies in so few chapters means that we can't go into great detail about many of them. These are a starter set; they give you enough foundation to follow up on your own. The competencies which we cover are grouped below. At the beginning of each chapter you will find checkmarks indicating which of them you will be exploring in that chapter.

CREATING MEANING   _____ Learning

UNDER PERSONAL CONTROL   _____ Thinking Reflectively   _____ Managing Goals
                                       _____ Managing Time   _____ Handling Stress

SOLVING PROBLEMS   ✓ Solving Problems

WORKING WITHIN SYSTEMS   _____ Being Interdependent   _____ Using Systems
                                         _____ Solving Systems Problems

WORKING WITH OTHERS   _____ Dealing With Others   _____ Working In Teams
                                         _____ Leading

PERSONAL TRAITS   _____ Adapting To Change   _____ Being Dependable
                                         _____ Taking Responsibility   _____ Acting Motivated
                                         _____ Acting Ethically/Honestly

Exercise 2A
WHAT'S THE PROBLEM WITH PROBLEMS?

We tackle problems constantly: at work, in school, at home, while driving, with our friends, at church, etc. A problem occurs any time we encounter a barrier which lies between us and where we want to go. Look at each of these situations from the perspective that there is a barrier to be overcome in getting somewhere:

◊ A driver waiting for a train to pass before continuing a trip.

◊ A student facing a math test, trying to complete 'Question 7.'

◊ A mother faced with three hungry children and little food in the house.

◊ Students charged with working as a team to complete a biology experiment.

◊ A businesswoman four miles from an appointment scheduled five minutes from now, with a police car driving behind her.

◊ An accountant faced with a malfunctioning computer thirty minutes before a major financial analysis is due to a key customer.

What results do these people want? A continued trip, a math answer, three satisfied children, a completed experiment, etc. In each case, there is a barrier between them and their goal: a train, math question, lack of food, etc. The fact of the barrier, plus the goal, cause the problem to exist. Not sure what that last sentence implies? Try answering these questions:

IF THERE IS NO BARRIER BETWEEN US AND OUR GOAL, IS THERE A PROBLEM?

IF WE HAVE NO GOAL WE ARE TRYING FOR, DOES A BARRIER MATTER?

Do the implications of that second question make sense? It is in fact true that we can have a problem only if we have a goal in mind. Right at this moment, somewhere, a student is sitting down with a tough math problem and a goal of finding the right answer to it. That student has a problem: a goal (right answer) and a barrier (unsolved math problem). On the other hand, I *also* have an unsolved math problem on the table beside me as I write these words. Do I have a problem? Nope, because I have no need to solve the math problem: I have no goal of getting the right answer. The 'barrier' of the unsolved math problem causes a problem for that student, but the same barrier does not cause me a problem at all.

> **A BARRIER CREATES A PROBLEM ONLY WHEN THERE IS A GOAL.**

Let's take a look at some common beliefs about problems. The statements below are perhaps true, false, or in between. Indicate how you feel about each statement by putting a check in one of the spaces beside them.

✍ BELIEFS ABOUT PROBLEMS: TRUE OR FALSE?

BELIEF STATEMENT	Strongly Disagree	Disagree	Agree	Strongly Agree
1. Problems should be solved in a short period of time.	_____	_____	_____	_____
2. The answer is what is important.	_____	_____	_____	_____
3. The best way to solve a problem is to jump right into it.	_____	_____	_____	_____
4. There are rules for solving most, if not all, problems.	_____	_____	_____	_____
5. Most problems have one clear right or best answer.	_____	_____	_____	_____
6. You can either solve a problem right off, or not at all.	_____	_____	_____	_____
7. There is almost always one best method for tackling a problem.	_____	_____	_____	_____
8. It is best to quickly pick one approach to a problem and see if you can force it to fit.	_____	_____	_____	_____
9. The problem which you need to solve is almost always obvious.	_____	_____	_____	_____
10. For math problems we mainly need to doublecheck our calculations.	_____	_____	_____	_____

How did your answers come out? Scattered, or all bunched at one side or the other? If you bunched them in the middle, you're probably trying to play it real safe. Or perhaps you're not sure *what* to think about these questions. In fact, the above ten beliefs are all mostly false. Not sure about that? Take some time and discuss why they are usually not helpful assumptions to make when you tackle a basic problem. You might think of situations where those assumptions are not true, where they harm your problem-solving efforts. Take #10 for example. What if you've interpreted or set up the problem wrong? Your calculations won't matter. The first key math need is to doublecheck your method or strategy.

Exercise 2B
WHAT KIND OF PROBLEM IS THAT ANYWAY?

Problems obviously come in all shapes and sizes. How to open a jar is not nearly as big a problem as how to put out a house fire. A subtraction problem is not nearly as involved as a calculus problem. Overcoming bad feelings after an argument is not the same sort of problem as fixing a broken engine. These differences are obvious once we stop and think about them.

But there is another kind of difference that is not as obvious, but is more important. That difference? The reality that there are different *types* of problems in terms of how we go about solving them. One useful perspective is to consider that there are two basic types of problems.

The most important difference between these two types of problems is the purpose for solving the problem: what are we trying to accomplish?

Remember what a problem is?

> A PROBLEM OCCURS WHEN THERE IS A BARRIER BETWEEN US AND OUR GOAL.

We can focus either on **getting to the solution now** or on **eliminating the cause for the future**. Let's examine the difference.

1. SOLUTION-ORIENTED PURPOSES

These problems focus on the immediate solution to a problem. Math problems are like this. Probably the majority of human problems are like this. We want to get over, under, around, or through whatever barrier keeps us from our goal. The businesswoman wants to get beyond the barriers of police car, time, and distance in order to get to her goal: being at her meeting on time. Here are examples of solution-oriented problem thinking:

◊ A student tries to clear the fog of tiredness from his head so that he can listen and take notes in class.

◊ A frustrated mechanic kicks a balky machine in frustration, hoping that it will start.

◊ A shopper, faced with a car that won't start, looks around for someone who might have jumper cables.

◊ A painter takes measurements before ordering some house paint.

What do all these situations have in common? A concern for getting to the immediate goal. These people are focused on the solution: getting good notes, a machine that runs, a started car, the right amount of paint.

How could it be otherwise, you ask? After all, *isn't the purpose of problem-solving to get where you want to go?* Well, partly it is. But let's expand that purpose. How about this:

> THE PURPOSE OF PROBLEM-SOLVING IS TO INSURE THAT YOU GET WHERE YOU WANT TO GO EFFICIENTLY, EACH TIME.

Those last three words add a lot. If taken seriously, they change the nature of your problem-solving work. Let's consider the situation of the shopper whose car won't start. What happens if she gets it jump started, then at the next mall it won't start again, and then later at home, and in the morning, and so forth? Getting it jump started again will achieve her immediate goal (getting it running so she can reach her next destination). But has it really solved the problem? This brings us to the other way to think about problems in terms of purpose.

2. Cause-Oriented Purposes

With this type of problem-solving, we focus not on the immediate goal to be reached but on the *cause of the barrier*. With the previous example, at some point the frustrated woman shifts to this type of problem-solving: looking at the cause and seeing what she can do to solve it. Let's watch (and label) her mental conversation shift:

◊   *"How can I get the fool car started?"*

is _____ oriented problem solving.

◊   *"How can I make sure this doesn't happen again?"*

is _____ oriented problem solving.

With the second question she has shifted to eliminating the cause of the barrier. Consider the implications of that shift for her actions:

◊   If her purpose is to get the car started, what's the easiest and cheapest way to accomplish it?

◊   If her purpose is to make sure the car keeps starting without help, what's the easiest and cheapest way to accomplish it?

Notice the result of her problem-solving. The "better" solution changes depending on how we frame the question. The more expensive and time-consuming action (perhaps 'buying a new battery') may not be the best choice the first time around. After all, it may not be the battery. After several experiences with no-starts, however, the easier and cheaper choice ('getting a jump start') may no longer be the best choice. Buying the new battery may become the best choice if it solves the underlying cause. The focus has shifted from reaching the goal towards preventing the barrier from occurring.

Or let's take another situation from the previous page: the student who is trying to fight tiredness in class. Notice how he can also deal with the situation as two different kinds of problems:

◊   *"How can I stay awake and concentrate now?"* is _____ oriented problem solving.

◊   *"How can I stop this from happening every day?"* is _____ oriented problem solving.

Notice also how the solutions differ greatly depending on how the problem is stated. What are answers to the first question? He can use many tricks to stay awake and concentrate now – moving often, pinching himself, etc. They're all useful in meeting his *immediate* goal. But they are not useful at all in solving the underlying cause, in answering his second question. They aren't helpful in insuring that he won't be in the same situation tomorrow. Useful answers to the second cause-oriented question might be things like going to bed earlier, getting up later, napping, eating better, etc. But those useful solutions to the second question do not help at all with the first, solution-oriented problem statement!

Actually, we sometimes use both types of problem-solving at the same time. For example, if your car doesn't start, your habit might be to say, "Let's see if I can get someone to jump-start it, then I'll drive over and see if the battery needs replacing." You've tackled both getting to the goal and eradicating the barrier at the same time. But, in fact, you've done this because you have simultaneously solved two problems: the goal and the cause.

With practice it becomes easy to identify which type of problem-solving you are doing. Let's have some practice now. On the next page make a check in the appropriate boxes to identify which kind of problem-solving each situation implies.

✍ WHICH KIND OF PROBLEM-SOLVING?

THIS SITUATION IMPLIES A FOCUS ON THE → → →	SOLUTION?	CAUSE?
1. This question asks me to define "alienate."	___	___
2. What is the square root of 645?	___	___
3. I'm worried that we are always over budget.	___	___
4. Darn it! This car is *always* hard to start on cold mornings! Here we go again.	___	___
5. Why do so many minority students feel alienated on this campus?	___	___
6. How can we keep Brenda from dropping out of school?	___	___
7. I have only $340 to cover $510 in past-due bills!	___	___
8. This machine is making scrap again, right at peak production time! How can I fix it now!	___	___
9. How can we best display the meats in these new display cases?	___	___
10. Have I got enough gas to get home?	___	___
11. Our sales are too erratic: sometimes way over and sometimes way under projections. That's got to stop!	___	___

You probably had some discussion (mental or with others) about some of those situations. For some of them it was not absolutely clear what level of solution the person had in mind. In the last one, for example, the speaker might have wanted to straighten out the immediate problem (perhaps by using fear as a tactic with his sales force?): a solution-oriented solution. Or he might have wanted to do an in-depth study of what really caused the variation and how best to change things to reduce the problem: a cause-oriented solution.

As mentioned earlier, most of us normally focus much more on the solution than the cause when we are solving problems. Think back to some of the problems you've solved recently and see if that pattern fits you. Then think about *why* you chose those solutions and see if you can answer this question:

✍ **WHY DO WE MOST OFTEN USE *SOLUTION*-ORIENTED PROBLEM-SOLVING STRATEGIES?**

Often we can expand a solution-oriented approach into a cause-oriented approach, just by thinking a bit more deeply about the situation and its implications. Below are some solution-oriented questions; think of a cause-oriented (deeper) question for the same situation. Sample answers to the first one are given.

1. **Solution-oriented**: "I've got to make up to her for my angry statements?"

    Cause-oriented: *"Why do I always say things before I can stop myself?"*
    or
    "What is there about the way she says things that always makes me angry?"

Note: Do you see how the second question focuses more on what causes the speaker to say things without thinking? And the third question focuses on what causes the speaker to feel angry in the first place. The answers to these questions may not help the woman feel better *this time*, but it may prevent the situation from arising as often in the future. Cause orientation.

2. **Solution-oriented**: "Out of gas again! Who can I call to come get me?"

    ✍ **Cause-oriented**:

3. **Solution-oriented**: "That's a surprising test question! How can I answer?"

    ✍ **Cause-oriented**:

4. **Solution-oriented**: "A last-minute order! How can we possibly get it out?"

    ✍ **Cause-oriented**:

5. **Solution-oriented**: "Where can I study to get away from that noisy kid?"

    🖎 **Cause-oriented**:

6. **Solution-oriented**: "I'm going to be late again. What excuse can I give?"

    🖎 **Cause-oriented**:

7. **Solution-oriented**: "Now I've got some big news. I know they'll listen to me *this* time!"

    🖎 **Cause-oriented**:

8. **Solution-oriented**: "That's the fourth time today that they've burned the french fries. They'd better not do it again!"

    🖎 **Cause-oriented**:

9. **Solution-oriented**: "Overdrawn at the bank again. I wonder if I can talk them into giving me another loan."

    🖎 **Cause-oriented**:

10. **Solution-oriented**: "Darn it. I can't find my car keys again! Where are they?"

    🖎 **Cause-oriented**:

Not every solution-oriented problem has a cause-oriented problem hidden within it. After all, if you're given a math problem on a test there's no reasonable action you can take to keep the next one from coming! But surprising numbers of our daily problems in school, at work, and in our personal life contain the seed of cause-type problems. If we don't work on them, they'll probably keep recurring and perhaps getting worse.

It's foolish to ignore the immediate problem in order to focus just on reducing the causes for the future. But it's probably almost as foolish to keep wrestling with recurring problems without also tackling the causes. Both problem-oriented and cause-oriented problem solving methods have their proper roles.

Exercise 2C
COMPARING TWO PROBLEM-SOLVING STRATEGIES

Defining the type of problem is one thing. Figuring out how best to solve it is another. The overall strategies for solving solution-oriented and cause-oriented problems are similar but not identical. You have to pick the right strategy for each type of problem-solving you plan to use. The differences between the two problem-solving strategies arise from differences in the kinds of questions you ask as you seek each type of result.

SOLUTION-ORIENTED STRATEGY

When you're doing solution-oriented problem solving (e.g. "How do I handle being late again?"), you're concerned with accomplishing a certain goal (e.g. being at work without being in trouble). Here's the questioning sequence you might use:

You're asking:	You're answering yourself:
1a. What's the goal?	To be at work without being in trouble.
1b. What's the barrier?	I'm already late; they get mad if I'm late.
2. How can I overcome that barrier?	Lots of possibilities: sneak in; lie; make an excuse; confess and hope they're in a good mood.
3. Which is best?	Let me examine the pro's and con's of each.
4. What should I do?	I'll try an excuse: the dog lost my keys.
5. How will I know if it worked?	By paying attention to their eyes and voices.

That line of questioning leads to the following general sequence of actions.

SEQUENCE FOR SOLUTION-ORIENTED PROBLEM SOLVING

1. *Clarify the problem (goal and barrier).*
2. *Identify alternative solutions to immediate problem.*
3. *Analyze alternative solutions to immediate problem.*
4. *Select preferred solution.*
5. *Test and doublecheck solution.*

CAUSE-ORIENTED STRATEGY

When you're doing cause-oriented problem solving (e.g. "Oh, no. I'm late again! I've got to stop this!"), you're concerned with the underlying cause of the barrier (e.g. "Why am I late so often?"). Your questioning sequence might be:

You're asking:	You're answering yourself:
1. What's the problem?	I'm late again and in trouble.
1b. What might be causing it?	Maybe I sleep too late, drive too slow, get up too late, or go the wrong way.
1c. Which one's the *main* cause?	Probably I allow too little time in the morning; something always comes up.
2. What can I do about it?	Get up earlier, or speed myself up after I get up, or cut down on my routine.
3. Which strategy is best?	I guess I'll try to get up earlier.
4. What should I do?	I'll set two alarm clocks, both twenty minutes earlier than I now set the clock.
5. How will I know if it worked?	By noticing what time I actually get up, and what time that method gets me there.

This line of questioning leads to this general sequence of actions.

SEQUENCE FOR CAUSE-ORIENTED PROBLEM SOLVING

1. *Clarify the problem (goal and barrier).*

1b. Identify alternative causes of the barrier.

1c. Analyze alternative causes of the barrier.

2. *Identify alternative solutions* to the cause.

3. *Analyze alternative solutions* to the cause.

4. *Select preferred solution* to the cause.

5. *Test and doublecheck solution* to the cause.

Notice that the shaded portions are the only differences between the two problem-solving sequences. But they are powerful differences.

✍ WHY IS IT IMPORTANT TO DISTINGUISH BETWEEN THE TWO PROBLEM-SOLVING STRATEGIES?

Below is an opportunity to practice distinguishing between the two strategies as they are practiced. Check whether each 'mental conversation' is solution-oriented or cause-oriented problem solving.

✍ SOLUTION OR CAUSE ORIENTED?

SOLUTION	CAUSE		
____	____	1.	"Let's see. I've got 110 miles to drive, my gas tank is a quarter full. At 30 mpg and a 16-gallon tank, I should make it. But if the gauge is a little bit off, then . . ."
____	____	2.	"This is the second time this month my fool son has called me, out of gas. Do I have time to go get Jim and still get to my meeting? But, more important, how can I break him of this habit? I wonder why it happens? Perhaps it's . . ."
____	____	3.	"Dad says that he'll have my head if I run out of gas again. What can I do to remember to fill it? I planned to get it filled yesterday, but then Rita and I got to talking. Speaking of Rita, I'd better call her. I'll try not to forget again so Dad won't be mad . . . "
____	____	4.	"I wish Bob and Jim wouldn't fight so much over the gas in the car. Of course I know Jim forgets a lot, and then calls Bob to come get him. How can I help my son remember? Maybe if I could keep him nervous about it. What if I covered over the gas gauge so that he never knew how much gas he had . . . ?"

Exercise 2D
SOLUTION-ORIENTED PROBLEM SOLVING

The remainder of this chapter explores solution-oriented problem solving. The special aspects of cause-oriented problem solving are covered in the next chapter. Solution-oriented problem solving is the most common type for almost all of us: something hurts *now* and we want it to stop! So we confront the barrier (of time, money, people, objects, or other things). We try to go over, around, or under the barrier in order to reach our goal. That goal, incidentally, is often to merely get back to the way we were before the barrier emerged (e.g. swatting the fly so we can regain our peace and quiet).

Let's consider some key characteristics of solution-oriented problem solving. A couple of spaces are left for you to add some other characteristics.

CHARACTERISTICS OF SOLUTION-ORIENTED PROBLEM SOLVING

◊　Focuses on getting to the goal.

◊　Is concerned with getting beyond the immediate barrier.

◊　Is relatively short-term.

◊　Does not insure that the barrier will not reappear.

✍

✍

ROLE OF 'THE CAUSE'

This type of problem-solving is not concerned with the **underlying** cause of the problem. It may, however, be initially concerned with the **immediate** cause. For example, when the shopper's car wouldn't start, she was concerned with whether or not a weak battery caused the situation. Overcoming the weakness of the battery (through jump-starting) was then the chosen solution to the barrier of a non-starting car. However, that's as far as her concern with the cause went.

Consider Eric. Eric walks into class late for the sixth time. The instructor says, "You're about to fail this course." Eric's got a barrier (about to fail) between himself and his goal (passing the course). With a solution-oriented problem-solving strategy, is he interested in the cause of the barrier?

Sure he is. *Why* is he about to fail? But, once he discovers that the cause of the barrier is his number of absences, he's finished with the cause. He tells himself to be on time for the four remaining class periods. If he can do it, he's solved the problem. But has he dealt with the *underlying* cause: his pattern of lateness? Probably not. Basically, this type of problem-solving only deals with the cause as necessary to solve the problem this time: not for the future.

When Useful?

Just because solution-oriented problem solving is not as long-term and permanent as cause-oriented problem solving does not mean that it is unimportant. It's the most common kind (by far), and it's probably the most important. How many cavemen were eaten by saber-toothed tigers while sitting around thinking about how to keep tigers out of their cave? Mostly we need to solve the immediate problem before or while we tackle any longer-term causes.

Below are listed some of the situations when solution-oriented problem solving is useful. See if you can add a couple to the list.

✍ Solution-Oriented Problem Solving is Useful When:

◊   Something hurts *right now*.

◊   The problem/barrier is unfamiliar.

◊   The cause is irrelevant.

◊

◊

◊

The previous exercise listed five basic stages in solution-oriented problem solving. Right now, *without looking back*, list those five stages (time to practice your information processing!).

✍ The Five Stages In Solution-Oriented Problem Solving:

◊   Stage 1 Is:

◊   Stage 2 Is:

◊   Stage 3 Is:

◊   Stage 4 Is:

◊   Stage 5 Is:

The next exercises explore each of these stages in turn.

Exercise 2E
STAGE 1 - CLARIFY THE PROBLEM

As we clarify the problem, recall that the problem consists both of the goal and of the barrier. Sometimes both of them are clear, but sometimes they aren't. There are at least four questions that can help you clarify the problem(s) you choose to tackle. They are:

QUESTION 1   What are my goals?

QUESTION 2   Which one(s) are most important now?

QUESTION 3   What are the barriers?

QUESTION 4   Which one(s) do I most need to deal with?

Does that sound too organized and systematic? For some problems, it certainly is. But we're not concerned here with the simplest, easiest problems. We're concerned with thinking through the fairly complicated ones that arise all the time. Let's take some examples from the life of Denise.

DENISE'S TALE: PART 1

Denise is tired and grumpy. She's worked much of the day, and had a full set of classes. It's hot in her apartment: air conditioning out again. She and her boyfriend have been having troubles for a while, and just had another big argument late this afternoon. She hasn't done much studying in a while, and the first round of tests is about due. Her head aches. It's after eleven, and her boyfriend is yelling at her. Denise says to herself, "If he shouts at me one more time, out he goes! For good!"

Let's analyze Denise's problem, using the four questions listed above. You will need to fill in some of the decisions as we go.

1 - WHAT ARE HER GOALS?

What does Denise want from this situation? It may be more complicated than you first think. To the right are some of the goals she might have:

◊   Peace and quiet at this moment.
◊   Good relationships with her boyfriend.
◊   Understanding of what's bothering her boyfriend.
◊   Freedom from her own tension.
◊   Her boyfriend trying to help her feel better right now.
◊   Time to concentrate on her studies.
◊   The chance to just get in bed and sleep.

2 - Which Goals Are Most Important?

It's your choice on this question. List one goal that you think *Denise* would say was most important.

✍ _____

_____

_____

_____

3 - What Are The Barriers?

Denise has a bunch of barriers in this situation, doesn't she? Just like she has a bunch of goals. Here are some of her barriers:

◊ *The physical/emotional impact of his shouting.*

◊ *Denise's own internal tension.*

◊ *The general relationship between Denise and her boyfriend.*

◊ *Their earlier argument.*

◊ *The late hour, at the end of a tiring day.*

4 - Which Barrier Does She Most Need To Deal With?

Again, your choice. List the one or two barriers you think are most significant in keeping Denise from achieving whatever goal you chose for her.

✍ _____

_____

_____

_____

_____

_____

So, What's Denise's Problem?

Take the goal you chose, and the barrier you identified, and make them into a statement of Denise's problem. It should take this form:

"The _(barrier)_ is keeping Denise from _(goal)_."

✍ **Denise's Problem Is That:**

Notice how important it was that you (a) thought about all the likely goals and barriers and (b) chose the most significant ones. Those thoughts and choices had a big impact on how you defined the problem. Which, in turn, will have a big impact on your solution. Consider some of the 'problems' you might have chosen:

◊ "The physical noise is keeping Denise from finding needed peace and quiet."

◊ "The tension Denise feels is keeping her from trying to figure out what is making her boyfriend so unhappy."

◊ "The argument earlier today is keeping Denise (and her boyfriend) from working on improving their relationship."

◊ "The heat and tiredness are keeping Denise from thinking clearly about what she should do."

DENISE'S TALE: PART 2

It's the next day, after a fight well into the night. Denise is at her job at McDonald's. It's lunch hour on payday. They are shorthanded, and have three new workers. The area supervisor is visiting – in response to some complaints. Denise has found out she has a surprise test tomorrow. She has already mixed up two orders. Now Mr. Lurch - a very familiar pain as a customer - yells to Denise over the head of some waiting customers that she's given him a soda that's flat.

Denise is having a tough time. Let's help her out, by helping her clarify the problem she's about to solve.

1 - WHAT ARE DENISE'S GOALS?
They might include such as these:

◊ Maintain her cool at the moment.

◊ Get Mr. Lurch straightened out with no more fuss.

◊ Don't make any further mistakes.

◊ Don't get criticized by her boss or the area supervisor.

✍

✍

2 - WHICH GOALS ARE MOST IMPORTANT?
✍

_____

_____

_____

_____

3 - WHAT ARE THE BARRIERS?
Some barriers to her goals are:

◊ Her tiredness.
◊ Shorthanded.
◊ Heavy lunch hour traffic.
◊ Pressure of area supervisor's presence.
◊ Already made two errors.

4 - WHICH BARRIER DOES SHE MOST NEED TO DEAL WITH?

Your choice of one or two barriers, depending on what goals you picked.

✍
_____
_____
_____
_____
_____

WHAT'S DENISE'S PROBLEM NOW?

Summarize your understanding of Denise's problem, based on your analysis. Use the format shown earlier.

✍
_____
_____
_____
_____
_____

DENISE'S TALE: PART 3

It's 8 o'clock that night. Denise is at home and wiped out. She got chewed out at work, and is too upset to eat, study, or anything. Her test is tomorrow, and since she had thought it was next Wednesday she has done almost no studying. It's the first test under a new teacher with a reputation for hard tests. Her boyfriend left a note that he was coming over later. It's raining . . .

On a separate sheet, clarify Denise's problem. Answer the four key questions:

1. What are Denise's goals?

2. Which goals are most important?

3. What are the barriers?

4. What barrier does she most need to deal with?

Then, as a final task, answer this question:

✍ **WHAT IS DENISE'S THIRD PROBLEM?**

Exercise 2F
STAGE 2 - IDENTIFY ALTERNATIVE SOLUTIONS

Once you've clarified the problem, you know two key things: where you want to be, and what key barriers are in your way. Only then are you in a situation where you can start thinking about what you can *do* about the problem. It may seem obvious, but answer the following question anyway.

✍ **WHY DO YOU NEED TO CLARIFY THE PROBLEM BEFORE IDENTIFYING ALTERNATIVE SOLUTIONS?**

Lots of people make mistakes by not clarifying the problem before they jump to a solution. The result? Often they solve the wrong problem. They reach a goal, but not the one that's really important. In fact, sometimes the goal they reach makes their real goal even more difficult to achieve. In solving a lesser problem, they put barriers in front of reaching their most important goal.

As an example, consider Denise's first situation from the previous exercise. She had several possible goals, and a number of barriers. We could have combined goals and barriers in many different ways, creating some very different problems. Four combinations which we identified were the following four problems:

◊ "The physical noise of her boyfriend's yelling is keeping Denise from finding needed peace and quiet."

◊ "The tension Denise feels is keeping her from trying to figure out what is making her boyfriend so unhappy."

◊ "The argument earlier today is keeping Denise (and her boyfriend) from working on improving their relationship."

◊ "The heat and tiredness are keeping Denise from thinking clearly about what she should do."

A key issue in Stage 2 becomes, think of alternative solutions to *which problem*? A possible solution to the first problem, about physical noise, might be to tell the boyfriend to either shut up or leave. That might eliminate the barrier.

But what if Denise's *real goal* is to improve their relationship? What effect would throwing the boyfriend out of the house have on *that* goal? The result of confusing a lesser (but emotionally tempting) goal with a greater goal is often to make the greater goal even harder to reach in the future. Poor problem-solving, caused largely by not clarifying the problem before considering alternative solutions.

How *do* we think of alternative solutions, anyway? This is by no means a science. There are no hard-and-fast guidelines. But here are some tips that might be helpful in thinking through the alternatives to a specific problem. There are a number of blanks included. Add your own ideas and other tips and suggestions.

SOME TIPS FOR 'THINKING OF ALTERNATIVES'

◊   THINK OF PAST ACTIONS

Recall what you've done in the past in similar (or different) situations.

◊   THINK OF OTHER'S EXPERIENCES

Recall what other people have told you that they did (good or bad) in such situations.

◊   IMAGINE OTHERS IN THE SITUATION

By mentally putting other people in the situation we can often reduce the emotional pressures which blind us to some types of solutions.

◊   THINK OF THE ABSURD

Often we 'censure' our own thoughts, and thus don't let ourselves consider certain types of solutions. Deliberately telling ourselves to imagine absurd solutions can help get over this difficulty.

◊   "IF ONLY I HAD . . ."

We often say or do something, and then later have better ideas. We can take advantage of this tendency by imagining ourselves the next day, saying to someone, "If only I had done/said . . ."

◊   PLAY OUT KNOWN ALTERNATIVES

Pick one option you can think of, and play it out. Imagine doing that, and examine the results. Often, when we see (in our minds) what we have done, we can then think of variations on that action which will work out better.

✍   _____

_____

_____

_____

✍   _____

_____

_____

_____

✍   _____

_____

_____

_____

✍   _____

_____

_____

_____

With these tips in mind, let's practice the fine art of thinking of alternatives. We'll keep picking on poor old Denise. Let's move on to Part 2 of Denise's tale. This is where she is working at McDonald's under all sorts of pressure and confusion. On the next page is one of Denise's problems. **Use the techniques on this page** to think of as many alternative actions as you can. Include dumb ones, too.

✎ **DENISE'S PROBLEM:** "Her tiredness and the fact of having already made two mistakes makes it hard for Denise to avoid getting chewed out by her boss and the supervisor."

DENISE'S ALTERNATIVES:

Did you think of a lot of alternatives? If you came up with more than **three** alternatives, you did well. How about other people? Did they think of many alternatives that you didn't? If so, ask yourself why that is so. Review the tips on the previous page again, and then tackle another possible problem.

✎ **DENISE'S PROBLEM:** "Mr. Lurch's embarrassing yelling, plus the heavy traffic, make it hard for Denise to keep her cool."

DENISE'S ALTERNATIVES:

Again, if you came up with more than three alternatives, you did very well! The best way to improve is to practice. Think about real or imagined problems, and use spare time (driving, sitting, etc.) to try applying these tips to those problems. Challenge yourself to steadily add more alternatives to the list.

Exercise 2G
STAGE 3 - ANALYZE ALTERNATIVE SOLUTIONS

Often we work on this stage while we are thinking of the alternatives (Stage 2). We think of a possibility and immediately begin to see how well it would work. Then this may lead us to consider other alternatives, similar or different (remember this as one of the tips for thinking of alternatives?).

What's the best way to analyze alternative solutions? There isn't one single 'best way' – we're all different, and situations are too different. So, once again, this stage is as much an art as a science. But there *are* a few tips which might be useful. Here are four of them.

TIP # 1 - ITEMIZE THE PRO'S AND CON'S

Almost any course of action has advantages and disadvantages. A useful strategy is to take one possible action, then say to yourself, "What are the advantages?" Go through them, and then repeat it with the disadvantages. This helps give you some general sense of which side outweighs the other.

TIP # 2 - MAKE A LIST

This third stage in solution-oriented problem solving can be very confusing. Why? You're got too much on your mind. You've overwhelmed the seven-item active memory room in your mind. You're considering possible goals, possible barriers, possible alternatives, and now pro's and con's. No way your mind can handle it all. You're dropping more out of active processing than you're keeping. So, if it's feasible, make a physical list: alternatives, pro's, and con's. If you can't make a physical list, at least try an orderly mental list. That will help some.

TIP # 3 - RANK THE CONSEQUENCES

Not all pigs are the same size. Likewise, not all consequences are equally important. When you are itemizing pro's and con's (hopefully in writing), you should also be noting which are the more important. Sometimes there can be many advantages, yet a single disadvantage can outweigh them all.

TIP # 4 - CONSIDER THE IMPACT ON OTHER GOALS

In Stage 1 you identified several goals, and chose to focus on one of them in your problem statement. But those other goals are still there, and many of them are important. A final tip is to weigh pro's and con's of a particular action in terms of how they will help or harm reaching some of the other goals. It's good to keep your options open on those other goals when at all possible.

Again, practice makes perfect – or at least better. Let's help Denise out some more by examining some of her alternatives. Since you identified some alternatives to help her out with her job problems, let's explore the pro's and con's of a few of them. On the next page is the clarified problem, plus several alternatives. Advantages and disadvantages are suggested for the first alternative. Add to them, and fill in the others.

✍ **DENISE'S PROBLEM:**   "Her tiredness and the fact of having already made two mistakes makes it hard for Denise to avoid getting chewed out by her boss and the supervisor."

DENISE'S ALTERNATIVES:

1. Concentrate hard, pretending that each customer is the last one.

   Pro's: *Breaks pressure into small parts.*
   Focuses on a main difficulty, which is concentration.

   Con's: *Doesn't help with mistakes already made.*

2. Double check each order TWICE before finalizing it.

   Pro's:

   Con's:

3. Apologize to the boss and supervisor for the two mistakes.

   Pro's:

   Con's:

4. Tell the boss you're sick and need to go home right away.

   Pro's:

   Con's:

There were many alternatives, weren't there? Remember the second tip? It was to write things down when feasible. Imagine laying out all the advantages and disadvantages for four alternatives *in your head!* No one could keep track of all that. Written down is definitely better.

Now let's try one more practice session, still helping Denise out. This time we'll switch to the third part of her story. Remember it? It's 8 o'clock at night. She's home, worn out, chewed out, underfed, with boyfriend about to arrive, and no studying done for a major test tomorrow. A hard test with a new instructor. A sweet situation. Here's one way to state her problem and a set of alternatives. The first one again has some advantages and disadvantages listed. You do the rest of the work.

✍ **DENISE'S PROBLEM:**   "Her exhaustion and lack of prior study don't make it likely that she will pass the test tomorrow."

DENISE'S ALTERNATIVES:

1.   Cram most of the night, then get 2-3 hours of sleep before class.

   Pro's: *Will at least have read over all of the material.*

   Con's: *Last-minute cramming is not very effective for processing or recall. May be too tired to stay awake for the test.*

2.   Sleep 3-4 hours now, then get up and cram until class time.

   Pro's:

   Con's:

3.   Call in sick and stay home.

   Pro's:

   Con's:

This page may underscore for you an important truth about examining the pro's and con's of your alternative courses of action. Sometimes there really aren't any very good alternatives. Sometimes you just have to choose between poor alternatives and bad alternatives.

Exercise 2H
STAGES 4 & 5 - SELECTING AND CHECKING THE SOLUTION

STAGE 4 - SELECT PREFERRED SOLUTION

Stage 4 of the problem-solving process doesn't require much explanation. Once you have examined the advantages and disadvantages of the best alternatives you have, you then do a hard thing: you choose an alternative. But there are a few aspects of that stage that you need to investigate.

Selecting a solution to implement is almost always a judgment call. There is seldom one solution which is *so* superior that it jumps out at you. Consider the alternatives that you just rated for poor Denise in the last exercise. They are summarized below. For both of the problem statements, **circle the alternative you would choose and explain why**. There is space for a new alternative if you wish.

✍ CHOICE # 1

DENISE'S PROBLEM: "Her tiredness and the fact of having already made two mistakes makes it hard for Denise to avoid getting chewed out by her boss and the supervisor."

DENISE'S ALTERNATIVES: (circle one):

1. Concentrate hard, pretending that each customer is the last one.

2. Doublecheck each order TWICE before finalizing it.

3. Apologize to the boss and supervisor for the two mistakes.

4. Tell the boss you're sick and need to go home right away.

5.

EXPLAIN WHY YOU CHOSE THAT ALTERNATIVE:

How likely do you think it is that the alternative you chose will do the job? In real-life, of course, you could do more than one of those alternatives, you wouldn't just have to pick one of them. How about Denise's second problem-definition? Fill it in below; add one if you wish.

✎ CHOICE # 2

DENISE'S PROBLEM: "Her exhaustion and lack of prior study don't make it likely that she will pass the test tomorrow."

DENISE'S ALTERNATIVES: (circle one)

1.   Cram most of the night, then get 2-3 hours of sleep before class.

2.   Sleep 3-4 hours now, then get up and cram until class time.

3.   Call in sick and stay home.

4.

EXPLAIN WHY YOU CHOSE THAT ALTERNATIVE:

This choice is an example of the type mentioned earlier: where there may not be any good choices at all. None of these three seem likely to do great things for Denise's standing in that course. What do you do when this kind of situation arises? Hope and pray. Do the best you can. And then switch to cause-oriented problem-solving, because these are often the very types of situations which you do *not* want to see again. To avoid them, you have to tackle the root cause, not just the instance of the problem.

STAGE 5 - TEST AND DOUBLECHECK THE SOLUTION

We've reached the final step in the solution-oriented problem solving process. It's a stage that every student has heard for years: check your work!

Did you realize that you could check on the wisdom of your decision about an alternative *before* you take the action? It's obvious that you can check it afterwards, but beforehand? How in the world can you do that? Read on.

You can check the wisdom of your decision before you take action by using two of your most powerful mental processes: organization, and imagination. Below are four techniques you can use to mentally test and doublecheck on your solution ahead of time. Notice how they mix creativity with mental organization.

Tip 1 - How Likely Is It, And Why?

Your subconscious mind often knows more than your conscious mind. Ask yourself to give a candid rating of how likely it is that your action will succeed in achieving your goal. If your frank assessment suggests strong doubt about the outcomes, then be alert. Back up and try to find another path.

Tip 2 - Re-Walk The Path

Simply retrace all of your thinking carefully. This whole process is like starting to climb a tree (the overall difficulty) and ending up on a specific branch: the best action to take to overcome the key barrier to reaching the key goal. You have left many branches behind you. Rethink your choice at each of those divisions.

Tip 3 - Where Could It Go Wrong?

Ask yourself this question: "*If* it goes wrong, *where* will it go wrong?" Your answer to that question will often give you a good clue as to which part of your decision to reinspect, carefully. It can also suggest how you can perhaps modify your chosen alternative a bit to minimize the danger.

Tip 4 - What To Look For

Ask yourself what specific results to look for, what specific signs of failure to seek. This can also suggest places to be alert.

Now for your final exam. On the past two pages you have made two choices for Denise. **Pick either one of those choices**. Write it below, and then check it.

✍ Checking Your Choice Ahead Of Time

Your choice was:

1. How likely is it?

2. Where could it go wrong?

3. What to look for?

Exercise 2I
PUTTING THE PIECES TOGETHER AGAIN

Solution-oriented problem solving has turned out to be a fairly elaborate affair, hasn't it? Five stages, and things to think about and do within each stage. In this exercise let's put the pieces back together. We will take a single difficulty and trace it all the way through from start to finish, using all five stages. This time though, let's give Denise a day of rest. We'll pick on Jerry. Jerry may be in too deep for anyone to help him, but let's see how well you do in helping Jerry deal with at least one important problem he faces.

NOT EXACTLY THE BEST TIME IN JERRY'S LIFE!

Jerry is an inventory control assistant at a local electronics plant. He's having a bad time. A new computerized inventory control system has just been installed. Because of some family problems (and the Atlanta Braves, his favorite team, playing in the World Series), Jerry didn't pay too much attention during those boring training sessions on the new system. After all, he's just the assistant!

*Not any more. Jerry's boss has been hospitalized and will be out for weeks if not months. Guess who's got to get the new system running? Even worse, he's only been there six months and is not even fully familiar with the **old** system (he exaggerated his credentials a little bit in order to get the job)! To add to his woes, the annual inventory inspection is scheduled for 6 weeks from now, and Jerry's already overworked because his boss is out. Then there's the problem of the $7,000 in computer chips that seem to be missing. No one can find them, but maybe they're in the warehouse somewhere. Unfortunately, there have even been rumors that Jerry stole them, since they've apparently disappeared since he came to work . . .*

STAGE 1 - CLARIFY THE PROBLEM

✍ What are Jerry's goals?

✍ What goal is most important now?

✍ What are the barriers?

✍ Which barriers does Jerry most need to deal with?

✍ THEREFORE, HOW DO YOU DEFINE JERRY'S PROBLEM?

STAGE 2 - IDENTIFY ALTERNATIVE SOLUTIONS

Use your definition of Jerry's problem, plus the tips discussed in Exercise 2F, to identify Jerry's alternatives. Try to come up with as long a list as you can.

✍

✍

✍

✍

✍

✍

✍

✍

✍

✍

Select the three alternatives that you think are most likely to be good ones. Write them, and the problem you identified, in the box below. Then list the pro's and con's of each alternative (using the tips discussed in Exercise 2G. Again, be as complete as you can – we don't want to get Jerry into worse trouble!

✍ **JERRY'S PROBLEM STATEMENT:**

ALTERNATIVE 1:

Pro's:

Con's:

ALTERNATIVE 2:

Pro's:

Con's:

ALTERNATIVE 3:

Pro's:

Con's:

Now is crunch time. Jerry's desperate, and he's come to you for advice. You're rushing out the door, so you only have time to shout out one suggested solution to Jerry. You hope it's one that will make his life easier, not harder. What do you suggest that Jerry do?

✍ **MY ADVICE TO JERRY IS THAT HE SHOULD:**

Later on, after it's all over, Jerry catches up with you at lunch. He tells you that he followed your advice. He tells you the results. Then he asks you this question: "What made you tell me to do that?"

✍ **WHY SHOULD JERRY DO THAT?**

STAGE 5 - CHECK THE SOLUTION

After you tossed Jerry your advice and rushed off, you got to thinking about what you had suggested. You double checked your chosen solution in your mind. What did you find out? Fill in your answers to these doublecheck questions.

✍ 1.   How likely is that solution to work?

✍ 2.   Where could it go wrong?

✍ 3.   What indicators do you look for?

Exercise 2J
ROADBLOCKS ON THE WAY TO PROBLEM-SOLVING

Sound problem solving isn't a particularly complicated activity, once you get used to it. However, too often people don't do it. Why not? Below are listed a few common roadblocks which get in the way of solution-oriented problem solving. See if you can add a couple more based on your own experience.

IMPATIENCE

When we face a problem, we often want to get it over with quickly. We are too impatient to think it through, telling ourselves, "That's a waste of time!"

FEAR

Solving a problem can be scary. It may take us into the unknown. Even more, it may take us where we subconsciously don't want to go. The best solution, for example, might be embarrassing. So we pretend that it doesn't exist.

ASSUMPTIONS

Assumptions are dangerous. If we're wrong about them, our analysis of alternatives can be way off track. For example, if we're mad at somebody it's tempting to assume that they are also mad at us. We choose our course of action on that basis. But what if they're *not* mad at us? Our answer may be wrong.

RUTS

"Drawing on past experience" is a very important way to create and analyze our choices when solving problems. But it has its weaknesses also. For example, because we've rejected a course of action in the past, we may be tempted to reject it again, without ever reconsidering its use in this new situation.

Exercise 2K
PROBLEM-SOLVING: MAKING YOUR MAP

An important part of this book is to help you map your current status and your goals as a mindful worker. In this chapter you've explored the competency of solution-oriented problem-solving. This exercise will help you to personalize what you have been exploring. Why? To help you to assess yourself as a solution-oriented problem solver and to see how you might improve and 'sell' your competence. Each of the next five chapters in this text will end with a similar exercise at 'making your map.'

Why do we call it 'making your map'? It helps you figure out three things: where you are, where you want to go, and how you might get there.

Your 'map' of the competency of problem-solving will consist of five elements: (a) brief descriptions of someone who is an especially competent problem solver (so you can see where you want to go); (b) your assessment of your current competence; (c) your goal in terms of how competent in problem-solving you want to become: (d) suggestions as to how you might improve your competence; and (e) suggestions as to how you might prove your competence in problem-solving to someone else (such as an employment interviewer).

Follow the steps below to make your map of your solution-oriented problem-solving competence. First, add two other characteristics of an exceptional solution-oriented problem solver in the "Someone Who" spaces in the box.

✍ PROFILE OF AN EXCEPTIONAL SOLUTION-ORIENTED PROBLEM-SOLVER: Someone who will react to a problem by systematically analyzing it. Who can step back and consider several possible alternatives. Who can cut through the confusion of emotions and uncertainty and focus on what needs to be done. Someone who can find creative ways to overcome barriers to their goal.

SOMEONE WHO:

SOMEONE WHO:

The person you have just described rates a "10" on the scale of 1 to 10. That person is really excellent at the job of solving solution-oriented problems. This description gives you a sense of the pattern of behavior associated with someone who is highly competent in this area: a target to shoot for in terms of your own competence. Use that description when taking your next map-making steps, on the following page.

Below is a blank 1-10 scale, with a 1 indicating horrible performance and a 10 indicating excellent performance. Think back to your work in this chapter. Consider how competent you are at solving solution-oriented problems, and how competent you would like to be. Then put two marks on the blank scale below, following these instructions.

a. Put an 'X' on the scale to show your *current* competence – how good you are now at solving problems.
b. Circle the number on the scale to show your *desired* competence. How good would you eventually like to be at solving solution-oriented problems?

✍ RATE YOUR OWN COMPETENCE AS A SOLUTION-ORIENTED PROBLEM SOLVER

HORRIBLE				FAIR					EXCELLENT
1	2	3	4	5	6	7	8	9	10

"X" point = current status   "Circle" point = 2-3 year goal

The final two map-making steps address two key questions about your competence. How can you get better at solution-oriented problem solving? And how can you demonstrate to other people your level of competence? The first question helps you move from your current competence (the 'X' point on the scale) to your desired competence (the 'Circle' point).

The second question helps you translate your competence into job-getting and/or promotion-getting skill. Remember that being good at something may not help you succeed in the workplace unless others know you are good.

To complete your map, fill in some possibilities in the two boxes below.

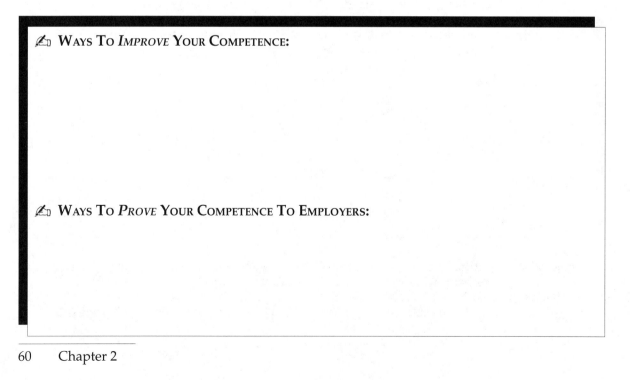

✍ **WAYS TO *IMPROVE* YOUR COMPETENCE:**

✍ **WAYS TO *PROVE* YOUR COMPETENCE TO EMPLOYERS:**

What do you now have? You've completed a personal map for yourself as a solution-oriented problem solver. If this competence is important in the high-performance workplace (which it is), then you now know where you stand, where you want to go, how to get there, and how to prove your competence. The rest is up to you.

Summary Of Chapter 2
IT ONLY HURTS WHEN I THINK ABOUT IT!

This chapter explored a lot of important territory about problem-solving: types, stages, methods, barriers, and the like. Think carefully, then list the most important things you want to remember from this chapter.

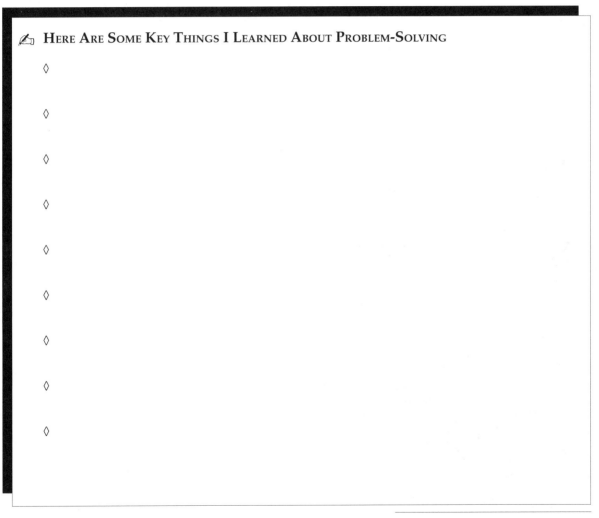

✎ HERE ARE SOME KEY THINGS I LEARNED ABOUT PROBLEM-SOLVING

◊

◊

◊

◊

◊

◊

◊

◊

◊

CHAPTER 2 – REVIEW QUESTIONS

1. Explain the relationships among a barrier, a goal, and a problem. Use examples.

2. Compare cause-oriented and solution-oriented problem solving: the similarities, differences, and why the differences matter. Use examples.

3. Examine the solution-oriented problem strategy: what are the stages, how they work, and why they are necessary.

4. When is solution-oriented problem solving useful?

5. Examine the key questions to ask when clarifying a problem. Use examples.

6. Examine four 'tips' for analyzing alternative solutions to a problem. Use examples.

7. When given real-world situations, be able to state them as solution-oriented problems and as cause-oriented problems.

8. When and why is solution-oriented problem solving important in the high-performance workplace? Use examples.

CHAPTER 3

EVERYBODY'S GOT A SYSTEM

MINDFUL WORKER COMPETENCIES
EXPLORED IN CHAPTER 3

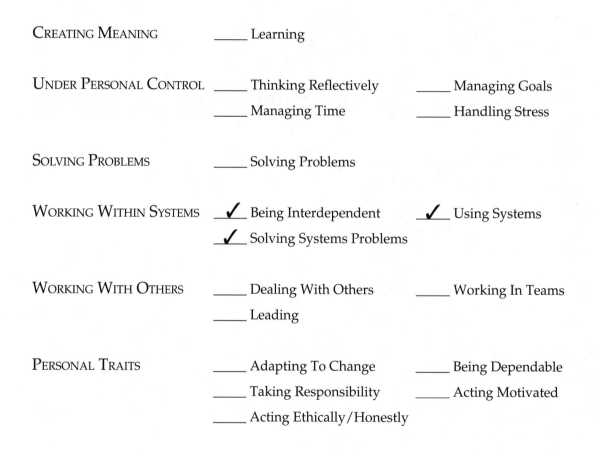

CREATING MEANING   _____ Learning

UNDER PERSONAL CONTROL   _____ Thinking Reflectively   _____ Managing Goals

      _____ Managing Time   _____ Handling Stress

SOLVING PROBLEMS   _____ Solving Problems

WORKING WITHIN SYSTEMS   _✓_ Being Interdependent   _✓_ Using Systems

      _✓_ Solving Systems Problems

WORKING WITH OTHERS   _____ Dealing With Others   _____ Working In Teams

      _____ Leading

PERSONAL TRAITS   _____ Adapting To Change   _____ Being Dependable

      _____ Taking Responsibility   _____ Acting Motivated

      _____ Acting Ethically/Honestly

Exercise 3A
INTERDEPENDENCE: WE'RE ALL IN IT TOGETHER

Many people, in all sorts of fields and concerned with all sorts of questions and problems, are rediscovering interdependence. They are discovering that building on interdependence may provide one of the most hopeful of paths into a very positive 21st century. The actions they are taking and advocating fit closely with the idea of the mindful worker. In many important ways, the mindful worker is a person who can work, learn, and contribute within an environment that calls for interdependence.

What is interdependence?   Simply the age-old idea that various things cannot work well (or at all) without other things. As the poet John Donne stated, "No man is an island." This is true for people. For machines. For companies. For government. And for entire towns and cities. Following are a handful from millions of examples of interdependence. Read them, and then add at least three of your own.

SOME EXAMPLES OF INTERDEPENDENCE

1. Floods in the midwest in the summer of 1993 caused farmers to sell their cattle, which lowered meat prices in New York for a while.

2. You can turn on your TV tonight because an engineer somewhere is at work, making sure that electricity flows to your house.

3. A faulty product coming out of one machine passes through two other parts of the production process, but then jams a third part because it does not fit properly into a slot.

4. Children of parents who read a lot usually enter the first grade eager and prepared to learn how to read.

5. A businessman chews his staff out because his alarm failed to go off and he was late for an important meeting.

6. You were able to go through a green traffic light safely because the other drivers all followed the same rules of driving.

7. A computer engineer knows how to design a computer which is twice as fast and half as expensive, but can't build it until another scientist can invent a piece of ceramic material with certain properties.

8. ✍

9. ✍

10. ✍

We have always been interdependent, of course. So what's different today? We are discovering that many of the toughest, growing problems we face can only be solved if we *deliberately* create and take advantage of interdependence. Let's look at an example of the need – and the change – in a little more detail.

INTERDEPENDENCE IN MANUFACTURING

BETWEEN COMPANIES

A company which manufactures something usually has to buy raw materials or sub-parts from other companies. How does it traditionally work? The manufacturer buys from a supplier who is cheapest, nearby, or something like that. Some of the supplies they get do not fit the requirements (specifications); this harms the manufacturer's equipment, leads him to produce inadequate products (which then break or don't work right when they get to you, the customer).

How do manufacturers traditionally deal with this? They hire people to inspect the supplies as they come in. Since some poor material usually slips through, the manufacturer still has problems in addition to a large payroll. In these times of fierce international competition, these manufacturers can no longer afford either the payroll or the problems.

How do wise manufacturers solve this very expensive problem? By becoming *even more dependent* on their suppliers! They make a deal with a chosen supplier. The deal? They tell the supplier this: "If you will operate in a way that guarantees that virtually all of your product meets our requirements, we'll give you all of our business, and a long-term deal." The manufacturer *also* says: "We'll help you produce more reliable stuff." Once the supplier accepts, and they work together to get the details worked out, the manufacturer ceases initial inspection and yet has few supply-caused problems. The supplier has a long-term deal (and a better product). The manufacturer has less payroll and fewer production problems. Everyone wins, because of *increased* interdependence.

BETWEEN WORKERS

This same thinking works *within* the plant. Let's say there are three workers in a sequence. Worker A mixes the materials. Worker B then molds them and Worker C fits them into a larger product. Worker C is always having to slow down, or produce unacceptable parts, because the material from B is sometimes wrong. Worker B has the same complaint about Worker A. Use the strategy of increased interdependence to reduce their problems. **What should they do?**

You probably decided that Worker C (with help from supervisors and other plant resources) helped Worker B to operate in a way that guaranteed a quality product from B. And Worker B did the same with Worker A. So B and C could quit checking the materials before putting them in their machine *without* worrying about producing poor products because of supply problems. Production went up, worry went down, quantity of defects went down, and costs went down.

This same strategy of increased interdependence is proving to be a powerful way to solve or reduce problems in many areas: school dropouts, drug use, health costs, economical housing, police protection, and on and on.

WHY IS INCREASED INTERDEPENDENCE SO IMPORTANT?

The answer to this question is straight-forward: many business, education, and community problems are impossible to solve *without* increased interdependence. Producing higher-quality products at lower costs, increasing the learning performance of all students, or reducing drug use, AIDS, illiteracy, or health costs can no longer be done by one group acting alone.

GLOBAL EXAMPLE # 1
REDUCING HEALTH CARE COSTS

Suppose you are a government agency or community group. You want to find a way to reduce health care costs throughout your community. Consider all the types of people who need to work together if that is to occur:

◊ Physicians, who set their fees.
◊ Drug companies, who make and price medicines.
◊ Insurance companies, who pay (or don't) for health care.
◊ Hospital administrators, who must keep facilities running.
◊ Lawyers, who handle malpractice suits.
◊ Patients, who demand help, "No matter what it costs."
◊ Government, who sets policies, rules, paperwork requirements, etc.
◊ And many, many other groups of people. All are interdependent.

✍ GLOBAL EXAMPLE # 2: REDUCING ILLEGAL DRUG SALES AND USE

List as many types of people as you can who need to work together on this.

Obviously it is impossible to expect to get *all* of these types of people together to agree on every decision relating to reducing health care costs or drug use. But it is equally impossible to expect major improvements in either area until most of them work together most of the time.

Let's switch now from global examples of the need for interdependence to immediate examples. Here are two of them.

Immediate Example # 1: Business Roles

Here are four jobs in a company. Traditionally they are not considered to have much to do with each other. Think beyond that. How are they interdependent?

◊   Line Operator - produces the widgets.

◊   Shipping Clerk - packages and sends the widgets to stores & customers.

◊   Marketing Director - advertises the widgets.

◊   Sales Representative - sells the widgets to customers.

Here are some examples of the interdependence among these people:

The sales representative depends on:

◊   the marketing director to familiarize possible customers with widgets.
◊   the shipping clerk to get widgets to the customers on time, undamaged.
◊   the line operator to make quality widgets, to keep customers happy.

The marketing director depends on:

◊   the sales representative to follow up and personally close deals.
◊   the shipping clerk and line operator for the same things the sales representatives depend on them for.

The shipping clerk depends on:

◊   the line operator to make quality widgets.
◊   the marketing director to design workable packages for them.
◊   the sales representatives to get orders correct, and in on time.

The line operator depends on:

◊   all three of the others to do well in order to protect his/her job.

These types of interdependencies seem obvious when outlined as we just did. But, unfortunately, many traditional companies do not yet notice them. Or, if they notice, they do not act on what they see. The marketing/design department may create a package for widgets which is attractive, yet which costs twice as much time (and payroll) to insert the widgets than some other design. Sales representatives may send in orders in a way that makes sense to *them*, but gives the shipping clerk fits. And none talk to the others to see what problems there are, and how they might work together to solve them. Lack of interdependence too often spells problems, increased costs, and poor customer service.

Here is another example. This time it is your job to find interdependence.

IMMEDIATE EXAMPLE # 2: EDUCATIONAL TEXTBOOKS

Schools are very dependent on the type and quality of textbooks. Here are some actors in the educational textbook drama:

◊ STUDENTS - who read the textbooks.

◊ TEACHERS - who teach from the textbooks.

◊ DISTRICT/STATE STAFF - who select the textbooks (K-12).

◊ PUBLISHERS - who pay for, package, and market the textbooks.

◊ AUTHORS - who write the textbooks.

List some of the ways these types of people are interdependent.

The *authors* depend on:

✍ _____

_____

_____

The *publishers* depend on:

✍ _____

_____

_____

_____

The *district/state staff* depend on:

✍ _____

_____

_____

_____

_____

The *teachers* depend on:

✍ _____

_____

_____

_____

The *students* depend on:

✍ _____

_____

_____

_____

QUESTION: How much do you think *these* types of people work together?

✍ _____

_____

_____

_____

Exercise 3B
SYSTEMS THINKING: APPLIED INTERDEPENDENCE

"Systems thinking" is a particular form of interdependence. Interdependence can be a very general thing, as you saw in the two 'global' examples in Exercise 6A. All of those types of people have a role to play in solving health care cost or drug problems. But they also have many other roles to play.

A *system*, on the other hand, is dedicated to a particular purpose. What is a system? It is a set of separate units which are designed to work together to accomplish a specific purpose. The units are sufficient and necessary to accomplish the target result. In an efficient system, you don't need any other units and you can't do without any of the ones you have. Here are some examples of some small and large systems. For each of them, list some of the units needed for the system. The first one is completed.

✍ EXAMPLES OF SYSTEMS

FOOD DISTRIBUTION SYSTEM: designed to get food from field to plate.

◊   *Units include: farmer, crop buyer, processor, storer, packager, shipper, retailer.*

COMPUTER SYSTEM: Designed to take in, store, and put out information.

◊   Units include:

EDUCATION SYSTEM: Designed to educate students.

◊   Units include:

HEATING/COOLING SYSTEM: Designed to heat and cool dwellings.

◊   Units include:

DEMOCRATIC SYSTEM: Designed to provide citizen-controlled government.

◊   Units include:

Most systems change over time: units added, units deleted, units changed. Consider some parts of the systems' units on the previous page which are no longer in common use, at least in the United States.

◊ Horse-pulled wagons are no longer part of food distribution.
◊ Blocks of ice are no longer part of heating/cooling systems.
◊ Key-punch cards are no longer part of computer systems.
◊ One-room schoolhouses are no longer part of educational systems.

What's been added? Airplanes and freeze drying for food distribution, laser printers for computers, heat pumps for heating/cooling, computers for education, televised coverage and national polls for the democratic system.

WHAT IS SYSTEMS THINKING, AND WHEN SHOULD WE DO IT?

A system has several key characteristics. It has several separate parts. These parts work together. And, together, they achieve things which none of the separate parts could accomplish by themselves.

"Systems thinking" means to look beyond your own unit and think of all of the units in a system. It's important to do this in at least three situations:

◊ When we try to *solve* cause-oriented problems (remember Chapter 2!).

◊ When we're trying to *improve* a system (even if there's no immediate problem).

◊ When we're trying to *understand* a system (oddly enough, there are many important systems that we don't even begin to understand. Think about the 'child development system' as an example).

When people are doing systems thinking, they are thinking beyond their own particular unit (role, function, responsibility). They are thinking about two interrelationships in particular:

1. HOW DO OTHER PARTS OF THE SYSTEM AFFECT THIS UNIT?

Remember the four types of workers whose interdependence we explored in the previous exercise? We were actually exploring this question when, for example, we recognized that the sales representative's role was heavily affected by the shipping clerk's ability to get the right number of widgets to the customer at the right time.

2. HOW DOES THIS UNIT AFFECT OTHER PARTS OF THE SYSTEM?

We would be dealing with this key question if we played the role of the sales representative, and realized that our pattern of sending in widget orders affected the shipping clerk's ability to get the orders filled for customers on time.

✍ **WHY DO WE NEED TO ASK *BOTH* OF THESE QUESTIONS IN SYSTEMS THINKING?**

Let's look at a more detailed example of these questions. Let's consider an ambitious young women who has just gotten her first job at a fast food restaurant – as a counter worker. Her medium-term goal is to be promoted to assistant manager, and she's heard that the best way to get promoted is to demonstrate that you can improve things. So, since she's read this book in the best course she ever had (!), she is trying to do systems thinking. Let's help her answer the two key questions, based on what we know about fast food restaurants.

✍ 1.   HOW IS THE COUNTER PERSON AFFECTED BY OTHER PARTS OF THE SYSTEM?

   2.   HOW DOES THE COUNTER PERSON AFFECT THE OTHER PARTS OF THE SYSTEM?

Improvements in a system can occur as a result of either question. But, very often, the best improvements come by asking them both. Why? Sometimes we can improve things within a unit. But more often the greatest opportunities to make improvements come in the links *between* units. **Why is that the case?**

✍

_____

_____

_____

_____

WHAT ARE THE CLUES TO SYSTEMS THINKING?

We're all in the habit of thinking only (or at least mainly) in terms of our own unit. Thinking actively and sensitively about our relationships with other units is often unfamiliar and uncomfortable. We need to be aware of whether we are doing isolated thinking or systems thinking.

> **The main clue to when systems thinking is occurring is by listening to what is being said (by us or others).**

Let's test your understanding of systems thinking — and your ability to identify its presence or absence when people are talking. Put a checkmark before any of the following statements which show system rather than isolated thinking.

✎ **TALKING ABOUT SYSTEMS THINKING**

SYSTEMS
THINKING?

___   1.   "You do your job and I'll do mine."

___   2.   "I think I've just created a problem for marketing!"

___   3.   "We need to get the three areas together and talk about this."

___   4.   "Engineering has messed us up again! Those guys are something else."

___   5.   "No way I'm going to tell you who my sources are."

___   6.   "Would it help you if we changed this form?"

___   7.   "Just fix it long enough to get through my shift."

___   8.   "I don't think we ought to go any farther until we check with the production folks."

___   9.   "I wish they'd get their act together. I'm tired of their foul-ups."

SYSTEMS THINKING IS POSITIVE

A key to correctly checking the above statements was to realize that systems thinking is a *positive* state of mind. You're not just aware of other parts of the system, you're interested in how they can fit together well. Just chewing out the folks in another department isn't system thinking — it's isolated thinking! You're concerned with them helping you, but not in a joint venture to improve things. Griping without positive action isn't systems thinking.

A KEY TOOL FOR SYSTEMS THINKING: FLOW CHARTING

Systems thinking is a state of mind and perspective. It is also a very disciplined way to make improvements and solve problems. When doing this, you can draw upon a number of very specific tools for helping you make the improvements and solve the problems. Several of these are covered in this chapter, to at least introduce you to some ways of thinking things through systematically. The first such tool is **flow charting**.

Flow charts are a kind of 'map' of a system. It shows all (or many) of the major units in the system. More important, it shows how they relate to each other. This lets you see how each unit influences, and is influenced by, the other units. Remember the example of the "educational texts" you did earlier in this chapter? A very simplified flow chart for that system might look like this:

What does this flow chart show? The 'flow' of events, in this case. The author unit writes. Then the arrow shows that this leads to the next event: the publisher unit's actions. Then the staff selection, and so forth. The student's studying the text is the last link in the chain. The author's efforts have 'flowed' to the student because of the efforts of the other units. There is no apparent need for an additional unit, and it appears that all of the units shown are necessary.

Improving a system with a flow chart requires you to look carefully at each unit and at the links between them. Consider the publisher's unit, for example. We could investigate how that unit does its job. How? First by making a flow chart of all the things that occur in the publisher's subsystem. At this level, though, we look at the relationship between the publisher unit and all the others. We ask questions like this: does the publisher's unit work in the very best possible way to meet the needs of the other units: author, staff, teacher, and student? If we can think of ways to meet those needs better, then we are close to making an improvement in the system.

Notice, however, that each flow chart is different, because the units and relationships to achieve one goal might not be quite the same as those needed to achieve a similar goal. Below, for example, are the four boxes needed to flow chart the system for selling popular books to individual readers who buy books in bookstores. Fill in the four boxes with the logical units of activity.

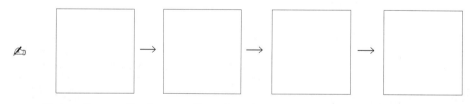

FLOW CHART OF SYSTEM FOR SELLING POPULAR BOOKS TO INDIVIDUALS

Notice how the two flow charts on this page are similar, yet different. And that difference is important. For example, suppose you were a publisher concerned with selling your book. In the first flow chart, you would explore the best way for you and the district/state staff to work together so that they would pick your book. You might be heavily into politics. But in the second case, the link between you and the next unit (the individual bookstore or chain) might be very different. Your systems and flow charts would be different in important ways.

The previous examples should have made clear how you make a flow chart:

◊ Identify the main units of the system.
◊ Put them in order.
◊ Link them with arrows.

Let's practice the whole process. In the blank box below (or on a separate page) create a simple flow chart of a 'student learning system' — the sequence of events from the time you walk in class until completion of the first test. Use about 5 or 6 units of action.

✍ **FLOW CHART OF 'STUDENT LEARNING SYSTEM'**

One final point about flow charts. Many arrows face both ways. That shows that each unit affects the other unit. Look at the textbook flow chart, for example. The way we drew it, it implies that authors write textbooks, submit them to publishers, and that's it. In fact, that's not true. Publishers often contact authors and ask them to write/revise texts. After submission, publishers and authors work back and forth in changing the text. The *actual* relationship between the two would look like this:

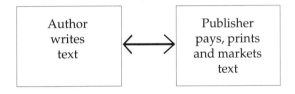

Why does this double arrow matter? With a single arrow, the publisher is only concerned with how they *receive* the text from the author. With the double arrow, showing that they reach out to the author, a whole new level of interaction (and possible improvement) opens up.

See if your flow chart needs double arrows. If so, add them.

This is only an introduction to flow charts, to give you a basic flavor for them. They can be much more sophisticated and powerful. If you're interested, you may want to follow up and learn how to improve them as maps of your systems.

Exercise 3C
CAUSE-ORIENTED PROBLEM SOLVING

Do you recall the two types of problem solving we explored in Chapter 2? We focused on solution-oriented problem solving: getting past a barrier in order to reach our goal. The other type was *cause-oriented* problem solving: focusing on the underlying cause of the barrier. That type will be the focus of the rest of this chapter.

Improving a total system requires focusing on the causes of problems. Let's take an example from our textbook system. What if an author sends a manuscript to a publisher, and the publisher loses it? Solution-oriented problem solving asks this sort of question: how do we get another copy of the manuscript? A good answer to that question might be to call the author and get another copy. That solves the immediate problem.

Cause-oriented problem solving, on the other hand, goes much farther. It asks a different question: what went wrong, and how can we make sure it doesn't happen again? Getting another copy of the manuscript does nothing to solve this problem. The solution lies somewhere in such areas as personnel training, procedures, equipment, and supervision.

Let's practice the differences in those questions a little bit. Following are some situations. For each one, identify an appropriate solution-oriented and cause-oriented question.

✎ SOLUTION- VERSUS CAUSE-ORIENTED QUESTIONS

A TV news reporter races to a phone to call a confidential government source on a very hot, rapidly-breaking story. The phone isn't working.

SOLUTION-ORIENTED QUESTION:

CAUSE-ORIENTED QUESTION:

A high-speed conveyer belt snaps during a production process, scattering very expensive, breakable parts across the floor.

SOLUTION-ORIENTED QUESTION:

CAUSE-ORIENTED QUESTION:

You're in the middle of an important work project when suddenly your boss erupts at you: "You're doing it wrong! Quit wasting time." She then stomps out of the room.

SOLUTION-ORIENTED QUESTION:

CAUSE-ORIENTED QUESTION:

You are stopped at a gas station. Someone points out that your front tires are very worn on the outsides. They are dangerous to drive.

SOLUTION-ORIENTED QUESTION:

CAUSE-ORIENTED QUESTION:

As you know, cause-oriented problem solving has a couple of extra stages. Below are the stages of solution-based problem solving. Shading is covering the additional elements in cause-oriented problem solving. Fill them in, either by remembering the shaded information or by figuring it out.

SEQUENCE FOR CAUSE-ORIENTED PROBLEM SOLVING

1. *Clarify the problem (goal and barrier).*

1b.

1c.

2. *Identify alternative solutions*

3. *Analyze alternative solutions*

4. *Select preferred solution*

5. *Test and doublecheck solution*

Exercise 3D
STAGE 1B: IDENTIFY ALTERNATIVE CAUSES

Stage 1 of both types of problem-solving was to "Clarify the problem," in terms of identifying and prioritizing both barriers and goals. This allowed you to state the problem in a form something like this: the problem is that this barrier keeps me from achieving that goal. We might state the problem in some earlier examples like this:

◊ The fact that we lost her manuscript keeps us from editing it.
◊ The fact that the phone is not working keeps me from talking to my confidential source.
◊ The fact that the conveyer belt is broken keeps us from getting those parts to the next part of the production line.

That stage is the same for both types of problem-solving. But then the two types diverge. Solution-oriented problem solving seeks to overcome the barrier: get the manuscript, find a working phone, fix the conveyer belt. Cause-oriented problem solving has some extra steps. Why? Because you do not yet know what underlying cause you need to fit.

To fix the cause of a problem, you first need to find out what it is.

The first step in that direction? Identify *possible* causes.

There are a number of ways to identify possible causes of a particular barrier. We're going to explore three of them: general questions, backward chaining, and fishbones. Here goes.

TOOL 1: GENERAL QUESTIONS ABOUT POSSIBLE CAUSES

Cause-oriented problem solvers, like skilled detectives, are equipped with a toolkit of questions which can help them find possible causes. Here are some questions which are often useful. You should add at least two others at the end.

QUESTION: WHO'S INVOLVED?

To find the missing manuscript, ask who handled it. For the broken conveyer belt, ask who installed it, maintained it, and/or operated it. **Vital note**: you are *not* looking for someone to blame; you are seeking allies to help you find the cause so that you can keep it from happening again. The best sort of cause-oriented problem solving, in fact, finds the source of a problem less in a person's actions than in their training, their equipment, policies, supervision, and other fixable things.

QUESTION: WHEN DID IT FIRST DEVELOP?

Often we can't get a good handle on a cause until we know something about when it first appeared. Did anyone notice the conveyer belt acting funny before it broke? When? How about the phone or the tire? Thinking back, can you figure out when your boss first started acting irritated about the project? Will that help give you a clue as to what went wrong, and why?

QUESTION: IS THERE A PATTERN?

Patterns are important clues to problems. Does the belt break often on this machine? How often? Does it break on all machines, or just this one. Remember Denise's problems? Is she just behind in her studying for *this* test, or does she have a pattern of being behind? Are telephones often not working? All telephones, or just certain kinds or certain locations? What's the pattern?

QUESTION: WHAT'S CHANGED?

It's often very helpful to see what, if anything, has changed recently. If there have been no problems for a long time, and suddenly there are a rash of problems, they may be caused by some change in the situation. The type of change can often be subtle: changes in the weather, changes in type of paint, changes in a phone company, changes in maintenance frequency. All can create unexpected barriers.

Below, list at least two other questions you might want to ask in uncovering the cause of some problem. Get ideas by thinking back to your own past experience. Then explain *why* they might help you find the cause of a problem.

✍ _____

_____

_____

_____

_____

✍ _____

_____

_____

_____

_____

Tool 2: Backwards Chaining

"Backwards chaining" gets its name because you start at the end (the barrier) and work backwards towards the underlying cause. Each step in the process forms a link in the chain of reasons. The key to backwards chaining? Ask *why*. Let's use the broken conveyer belt as an example. We start by asking why the result occurred. Then for each answer we ask why *that* occurred. It looks like this:

Example Of Backward Chaining

Ask "Why?"	The Answer
1. Why are the parts scattered on the floor?	Because the conveyer belt broke.
2. Why did the conveyer belt break?	It looks like the clamp came loose where the two ends meet.
3. Why did the clamp come loose?	The bolt holding the clamp in place fell out.
4. Why did the bolt fall out?	Because the nut came off the end.
5. Why did the nut come off?	Maybe it loosened gradually.
6. Why did it loosen gradually?	Because no one tightened it every once in a while.
7. Why didn't someone tighten it?	It's not anybody's job to do that.
8. Why isn't it anybody's job?	I guess no one ever thought it was important.
9. Why didn't anyone think it was important?	Because the belts on the old machine were welded.

Notice how easy that process was. Each answer suggested the next "Why" question to ask. Sometimes it's not that tidy, but very often all you have to do is keep asking, "Why?" until the answer reveals itself. Notice two other important things about what happened in this backwards chain.

1. No one got blamed personally. Maintenance man, operator, supervisor, etc., were part of a system, and it was the *system* that failed.

2. Ultimately, the problem got traced back to a *change*. In this case, new machinery was installed and no one thought to notice a very minor but eventually important difference in the new machinery.

Now it's your turn to do a backwards chain. Let's continue exploring the mystery of the lost manuscript. The author put it in the mail. The editor does not have it when the time comes to go to work (though everyone agrees that it got to the publisher's offices). Use your imagination and create a 5-7 step chain of causes behind causes.

✍ THE MYSTERY OF THE MISSING MANUSCRIPT

ASK "WHY?"   THE ANSWER

1.   I can't edit the manuscript.   ⟶   I don't have it here.

Here are some more practice situations:

1.   "I got a poor grade."   *Why?*   "I didn't study."

2.   "I can't buy that."   *Why?*   "I spent all my money."

3.   "I feel terrible!"   *Why?*   "I hurt someone with my words."

TOOL 3: FISHBONES

You have your choice of things to call this technique. You can call it an Ishikawa diagram. Or you can call it a fishbone. 'Fishbone' may be a little easier to remember for most of us — and it will also help you remember how the technique works.

A fishbone is a way to both generate and organize ideas about the causes of a problem. People have discovered that most causes of problems are of four types:

◊ EQUIPMENT CAUSES - car, drill press, computer, stove, VCR, etc.

◊ MATERIAL CAUSES - oil, metal, disk, food, tape, etc.

◊ METHOD CAUSES - wrong instructions for installing oil filters, programming the computer, etc.

◊ PEOPLE PROBLEMS - mistakes, lack of knowledge or training, etc.

You draw a fishbone like the one below, with the problem written at the end and four separate 'bones' for the four major cause areas:

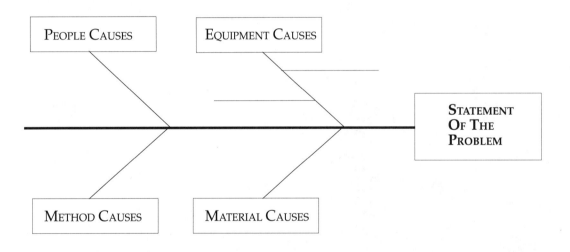

When using a fishbone chart, you look at the problem and then ask, "What equipment factors might possibly have caused the problem?" See the couple of smaller 'bones' sticking off of the equipment bone? You draw bones like those for each *possible* cause that you can think of.

You then repeat that procedure for material, then methods, and then people. As you're working in one area, you may think of another possible cause in another area: add it on where it fits. The idea is to think of **as many possible causes** as you can, and put each one on a 'bone.'

Here is part of a completed fishbone. The problem this time is persistently bad coffee. Notice how there are a couple of bones for each of the four main types of causes. **See if you can add some other possible causes of bad coffee**.

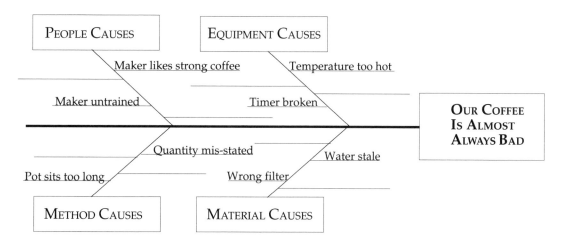

Notice how many possible causes you identified using this method. It's a powerful tool for use in this stage of cause-oriented problem solving. By the way, don't worry if you can't decide whether a cause belongs in one category or another (for example, 'maker untrained' could be a people cause or a method cause). Put it under either category; just be sure it's on some bone.

Let's close this section with one final practice. See how many causes you can add to this fishbone. The problem: I failed my second chemistry test in a row.

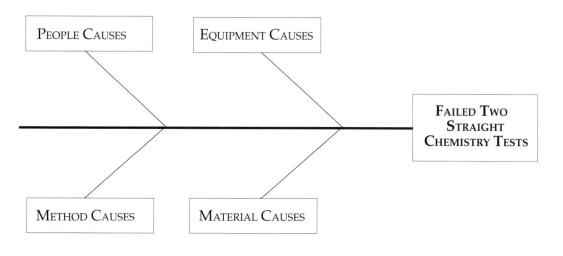

Exercise 3E
STAGE 1C: ANALYZE POSSIBLE CAUSES

Stage 1b hopefully identified all of the likely causes of a particular problem. With stage 1c we want to narrow it down a bit, and decide **what is the most** **likely or important cause** of the problem. Why is this important? Your answer:

✎ WHY IS IT IMPORTANT TO IDENTIFY THE MOST LIKELY/IMPORTANT CAUSE?

High performance businesses and industries have perhaps made the greatest breakthroughs in their problem-solving methods in this stage of the process. To figure out why, let's look at the various ways in which we often decide what cause to concentrate on. Here are some ways to analyze the main cause of a problem, using Denise's pattern of last-minute studying as an example.

WAYS TO ANALYZE THE MAIN CAUSE OF A PROBLEM

USE HARD DATA
Go out and collect solid information about how often each possible cause seems to be the reason for the problem.

Example: *"Let's see how often Denise went out instead of studying."*

USE PAST EXPERIENCE
Recall what you have done yourself, or what you have experienced with that problem.

Example: *"If it's after ten, I usually say 'to heck with studying.'"*

USE LOGIC
Analyze various aspects logically: human behavior, likely patterns, cause and effect, and so forth.

Example: *"It seems logical that she's spending too much time with her boyfriend, plus working."*

USE VALUES
Apply your own values, beliefs, and prejudices to decide what's really causing the problem.

Example: *"See what I told you! Full-time students should never try to work at the same time! Look what happened."*

There are other ways to sort through the possible causes of a problem. **Tradition** ("That's always been the problem."), **intuition** ("I've got a feeling that . . ."), or **expediency** ("Quick, do something!") are examples. Think about all those methods, and answer this question:

✎ WHICH METHOD REPRESENTS A ' BREAKTHROUGH' FOR MODERN BUSINESSES?

Strange as it may seem, traditional businesses have not done a very good job of using information effectively in uncovering the fundamental cause of problems. This has been true even of major problems. Too often, businesses have used a 'quick-fix' method (basically, solution-oriented problem solving) and have not rigorously examined and compared possible causes. A serious focus on getting and using information to identify main causes of persistent problems is one of the single biggest breakthroughs for many high performance businesses. The rest of our exploration of Stage 1c will concentrate on using information to analyze causes.

COMMON MISTAKES WHEN COLLECTING & USING INFORMATION

Americans don't seem to like to spend much time collecting information before 'jumping to a conclusion.' That's the judgment made by many people who have compared the United States with other countries in terms of problem-solving patterns. We seem to want to 'get to the meat of the thing,' and tend to be impatient with "wasting time" by collecting lots of information. One result is that when we do set out to collect and use information we find it easy to make mistakes. Here are four of the more common mistakes we need to avoid.

FOUR COMMON MISTAKES

1. NOT REALIZING THAT USEFUL INFORMATION CAN BE GATHERED.
    We don't stop and think about what information we might want, and how we can get it. We drop out before even starting.

2. COLLECTING THE WRONG INFORMATION.
    We don't think twice about what information we collect and how it fits. Often we just get whatever information is easiest, whether it fits or not!

3. NOT COLLECTING SUFFICIENT INFORMATION.
    We get what we can, and then stop. We take the easy way out.

4. MISINTERPRETING INFORMATION.
    We organize our information poorly, or we twist, misunderstand, or otherwise misinterpret it.

Let's apply those four mistakes to Denise's case. You're her friend, and are trying to help her figure out the underlying cause of her pattern of not starting to study until too late. Being well-trained in traditional business methods, you immediately make all four common mistakes. Below, **think creatively of statements you might make** if you were making each of those mistakes while 'helping' Denise. One example is given.

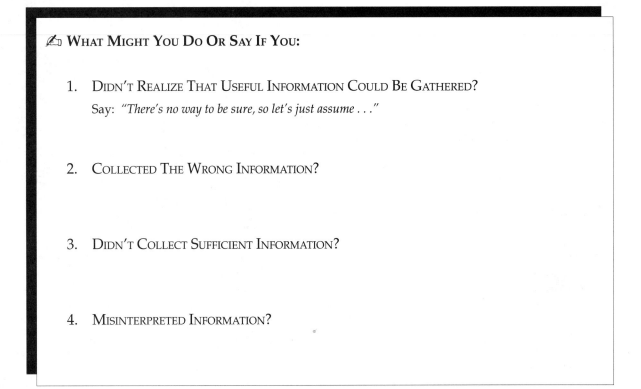

✍ WHAT MIGHT YOU DO OR SAY IF YOU:

1. DIDN'T REALIZE THAT USEFUL INFORMATION COULD BE GATHERED?

    Say: *"There's no way to be sure, so let's just assume . . ."*

2. COLLECTED THE WRONG INFORMATION?

3. DIDN'T COLLECT SUFFICIENT INFORMATION?

4. MISINTERPRETED INFORMATION?

If we think back frankly into our own patterns of solving problems, we'll realize that these kinds of mistakes aren't just committed by traditional businesses. They are very common factors in our own problem solving. The remainder of this exercise focuses on two tools which help avoid those problems: distribution analysis and Pareto charts. Both are very powerful, simple ways to collect and use information in order to identify the most important cause(s) of a problem.

TOOL # 1: DISTRIBUTION ANALYSIS

Professional sports teams and TV sports announcers could give all of us lessons in using the tool of distribution analysis. They do it all the time. Have you ever watched a baseball game on TV and the announcer has shown a picture of the baseball field, with little "x"s where each hit has landed? Or a football game with "x"s for where passes have been thrown? Or basketball with "x"s where shots have been taken? You've been watching distribution analysis in action.

If you're not into sports, have you read a report in the paper that said something like, "Officials have put up a traffic light on the corner of Bright Street and Dark Avenue, because 31% of the serious accidents in the county in the past year have occurred at that intersec- tion"? The city officials have been doing some distri- bution analysis.

Based on those two examples, and the name, you should be able to answer this:

✍ "DISTRIBUTION ANALYSIS" MEANS:

Oddly enough, for many years most businesses and industries did not make great use of this very simple tool. They might notice that sales were down, or returned products were up, or production seemed erratic within a plant. But they did not go farther than that. They did not tend to get information on the distribution pattern of where the problem occurred

so that they could analyze it. The information was available, but they did not get or use it.

Let's take the Mudhen Sneaker Company as an ex- ample. Here's their tale. At the end of it, suggest what information they should gather.

✍ THE TALE OF THE MUDHEN SNEAKER COMPANY

*The Mudhen Sneaker Company last year introduced a new line of basketball shoes, named for a famous professional player: Jumper McScoot. At first the shoes sold so well that they couldn't keep up with the demand. In communities all over the country they were the number one seller. At first. But then the troubles began. The flow of shoes **out** to stores started to be matched by the flow of shoes **back** into the company, as flawed rejects. The shoes weren't holding up. Kids started calling them "Jumper McJunks."*

*Mudhen had too much invested to quit. They doubled inspection at the plant. They tripled advertising. They offered rebates. Nothing seemed to work. Desperate, they hired you as a consultant. **What action do you suggest that they take to figure out the main cause of the problem?***

Hope you earned your $7,500 consulting fee by giving the Mudhen Sneaker Company some good advice. They sure didn't need to lose any more money! And you probably did do the right thing, by asking them to analyze where the sneakers were breaking down. Toe? Sole? Lace holes? Heel? Sides? There's not much chance of their figuring out what caused all the rejects until they figured out where they were occurring. Once that's done, then they can really get down to business.

That is, in fact, a realistic situation. Many companies, faced with growing amounts of rejects, failed to clarify what part of the product was failing. Without a distribution analysis, they will have a tough time finding the cause.

Sounds like an easy solution, doesn't it? Often it is. But sometimes it requires a little thinking to decide *distribution of what*? For example, consider a company that manufactured expensive pens. These pens started being returned by angry customers at an increasing rate.

For writing pen rejects, they might want to check the distribution of:

◊ What kind of fault (leaks, falls apart, scratched, etc.)?
◊ Where it was made? (Which plant? Which production line in the plant?)
◊ What kind of use it had? (Much/little? Indoor/outdoor?)
◊ Where it was used (hot climate, dry climate, cold climate)?

Any of these factors might help solve the problem. For example, they might eventually decide that the pens leaked when used heavily in cold outdoor climates. The solution (a different ink?) would be very different than if the problem was that they got scratched easily all the time (a different finish?).

Consider the following situations. For each one, see if you can think of several types of distribution that you might want to investigate.

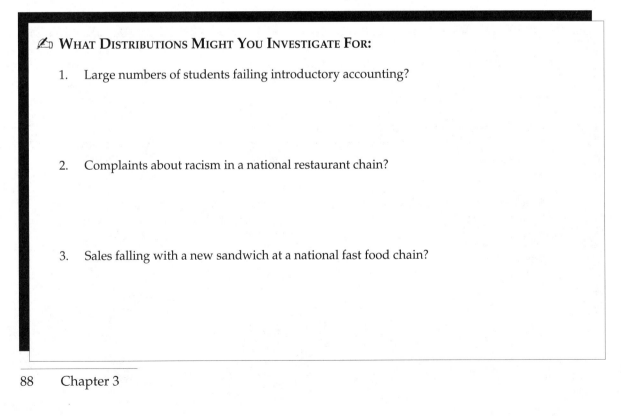

✍ **WHAT DISTRIBUTIONS MIGHT YOU INVESTIGATE FOR:**

1. Large numbers of students failing introductory accounting?

2. Complaints about racism in a national restaurant chain?

3. Sales falling with a new sandwich at a national fast food chain?

Avoiding common information-gathering problems and doing distribution analyses go a long way towards analyzing the most important cause of a problem. The final technique in this segment helps you figure out what to do with the distribution data once you have it.

Tool # 2: Pareto Charts

Unlike fishbones (also known as Ishikawa Diagrams), there is no shorthand, descriptive name for a Pareto Chart. You'll just have to remember it. You *might* want to remember the Pareto rule: the 80/20 rule. That rule says that 20 percent of one thing causes 80 percent of another thing. Examples:

◊ in marketing, 20% of the customers generate 80% of the sales;
◊ in research, 20% of the researchers make 80% of the discoveries;
◊ in purchasing, 20% of the buyers make 80% of the purchases; and
◊ in politics, 20% of the voters influence 80% of the laws.

Of course, these figures are not exact, but they do make an important truth: a relatively few causes account for a great percentage of the results. In terms of this chapter, how would you state a Pareto rule for systems problems? Fill in the blanks below.

✍ In systems 20% of the _____ account for 80% of the _____.

Pareto charts graphically display the results of that rule. How? By using a *bar chart* to show the results of your distribution analyses. It compares causes with frequency. For example, The Mudhen Sneaker Company (with your help) finally wised up. They took a count of the type of defect in each returned sneaker. They then translated those numbers into percentages. They then put the percentages on a bar chart of the causes of defects in Jumper McScoot tennis shoes compared to the number of times each defect happened. The Pareto bar chart for McScoots might look like the one below.

	PERCENTAGE OF TOTAL DEFECTS								
DEFECT	5	10	15	20	25	30	35	40	45
LOOSENED SOLES	XXXXXXXXXXXXXXXXXXXXXXXXXXXXXXXXXXXXXXXXXXX								
SEPARATED SIDES	XXXXXXXXXXXXXXXXXXXXXXXXXXXXXX								
TORN LEATHER	XXXXXXXXX								
SPLIT BACK	XXXX								
CRACKED SOLE	XXXX								
FADED LEATHER	XXX								
5 OTHER DEFECTS	XX								

What does that Pareto chart tell us? The 'bar' beside the top defect (loosened soles) goes out to about 43%. When they inspected the returned shoes, they found that 43% of them had loose soles. The second bar (separated sides) accounted for about 30% of the defects. Then a sharp drop to torn leather (10%) and a few other items.

Notice what the Mudhen Sneaker Company (with your assistance, of course) has learned. About 73% of the rejects were for only two reasons (close enough to the Pareto 80/20 principle). Notice also how similar the two problems were: loosened soles and separated sides. When they investigated, they found that the culprit was the kind of glue they were using: it didn't do the job. Changing the glue solved almost three-quarters of the problem, putting McScoot's back into the market (and keeping Mudhen in business). Distribution analysis plus Pareto charts did the job. You earned your $7,500 fee!

Your turn to do a Pareto chart. This time you can use the distribution analysis data from the 'poor coffee' study. Here's what they learned upon checking.

Frequency of causes of poor coffee at Markemup's fast food chain:

◊   Stale water - 523 times.
◊   Timer broken - 191 times.
◊   Dirty coffee pot - 1,211 times.
◊   Coffee maker untrained - 6,294 times.
◊   'Made' coffee sits too long - 4,732 times.
◊   Burner malfunctions - 286 times.
◊   Wrong quantity used - 603 times.
◊   27 other causes - 940 times.

To close this exercise, make a Pareto chart of this coffee data.

PROBLEM	PERCENTAGE OF ERRORS								
	5	10	15	20	25	30	35	40	45
◊									
◊									
◊									
◊									
◊									
◊									
◊									
◊									

Based on this organized information, what should Markemup's do to solve the problem of consistently bad coffee?

Exercise 3F
THE SEVEN STAGES OF CAUSE-ORIENTED PROBLEM-SOLVING

We've covered the first three stages of cause-oriented problem solving. The other four are just like those you worked on in the previous chapter, except that your target is removal or reduction of the *cause* itself rather than just the short-term barrier. It's important that you become and *remain* familiar with those seven stages. They will be a very important part of a mindful worker's competence. Here are those seven stages once again. As a refresher, for each one **note the tasks, tips, and tools** we have discussed for each stage in this chapter and the previous chapter.

✍ **TIPS FOR THE SEVEN STAGES OF CAUSE-ORIENTED PROBLEM-SOLVING**

1. Clarify the problem:

    Identify and prioritize the goals and the barriers.
    State the problem.

1b. Identify alternative causes of the barrier:

1c. Analyze alternative causes of the barrier:

2. Identify alternative solutions to the cause:

3. Analyze alternative solutions to the cause:

4. Select preferred solution to the cause:

5. Test and doublecheck solution to the cause:

For the rest of this exercise you are going to walk through all seven stages of cause-oriented problem solving. **You will start by creating a situation: a complex, realistic, persistent problem**. You will then work that problem through one stage at a time. If you need to create more details of the situation as you go, make them up. You will need to create some data (e.g. for your distribution analysis). Make that up also. Let's see where your problem-solving leads.

On a separate page, write out the problem and give it a title. Then complete these stages of cause-oriented problem solving.

STAGE 1: CLARIFY THE PROBLEM

✍ Given my analysis, I would state the problem this way:

_____

_____

_____

_____

STAGE 1B: IDENTIFY ALTERNATIVE CAUSES

✍ The alternative causes I found were:

_____

_____

_____

_____

✍ The methods I used to identify alternative causes were:

_____

_____

_____

_____

1C: ANALYZE ALTERNATIVE CAUSES

✍ The pros/cons of several alternative causes were:

_____

_____

_____

_____

✍ The methods I used to analyze the alternative causes were:

_____

_____

_____

_____

✍ Based on my analysis, I think the main cause of the problem is:

_____

_____

_____

_____

STAGE 2: IDENTIFY ALTERNATIVE SOLUTIONS TO THE MAIN CAUSE

✎ The alternative solutions I found were:

_____

_____

_____

_____

✎ The methods I used to identify alternative solutions were:

_____

_____

_____

STAGE 3: ANALYZE ALTERNATIVE SOLUTIONS TO THE MAIN CAUSE

✎ The pros/cons of the alternative solutions were:

_____

_____

_____

_____

✎ The methods I used to analyze alternative solutions were:

_____

_____

_____

_____

STAGE 4: SELECT PREFERRED SOLUTION TO THE MAIN CAUSE

✎ Based on my analysis, I judge that the best solution is:

_____

_____

_____

_____

STAGE 5: TEST AND DOUBLE CHECK SOLUTION TO THE MAIN CAUSE

✎ Test the preferred solution:

_____

_____

_____

_____

✎ The methods I used to decide how to test and double check my solution are:

_____

_____

_____

_____

✎ What are the hardest parts of these stages? How will you remember them?

_____

_____

_____

Exercise 3G
Systems: Making Your Map

✍ PROFILE OF SOMEONE WHO CAN BE EXCEPTIONALLY INTERDEPENDENT: Someone who focuses not just on themselves but also on the problems, needs, and roles of those around them. Someone who makes decisions based as much on 'the common good' as on personal desires. Someone who tries hard to help other people understand and act on our interdependence.

Someone who:

Someone who:

✍ RATE YOUR OWN COMPETENCE AT BEING INTERDEPENDENT

HORRIBLE				FAIR					EXCELLENT
1	2	3	4	5	6	7	8	9	10

"X" point = current status   "Circle" point = 2-3 year goal

✍ **WAYS TO *IMPROVE* YOUR COMPETENCE:**

✍ **WAYS TO *PROVE* YOUR COMPETENCE:**

✍ PROFILE OF AN EXCEPTIONAL SYSTEM USER: Someone who can look at an event or action and see a long chain of other related events or actions. Who can look at one person's role and see how it fits with many other roles.

Someone who:

Someone who:

✍ RATE YOUR OWN SYSTEM-USING COMPETENCE

HORRIBLE				FAIR					EXCELLENT
1	2	3	4	5	6	7	8	9	10

"X" point = current status   "Circle" point = 2-3 year goal

✍ WAYS TO *IMPROVE* YOUR COMPETENCE:

✍ WAYS TO *PROVE* YOUR COMPETENCE:

✍ Profile Of An Exceptional Cause-Oriented Problem Solver: Someone who can trace a problem back to its fundamental roots. Who can use cause-and-effect thinking to find the causes of things, and can then pin down the key cause.

Someone who:

Someone who:

✍ Rate Your Own Competence As A Cause-Oriented Problem Solver

Horrible				Fair					Excellent
1	2	3	4	5	6	7	8	9	10

"X" point = current status   "Circle" point = 2-3 year goal

✍ Ways To *Improve* Your Competence:

✍ Ways To *Prove* Your Competence:

Summary Of Chapter 3
EVERYBODY'S GOT A SYSTEM!

This chapter covered three very significant topics: interrelationships, systems thinking, and cause-oriented problem solving. What are the most important things you got from the chapter?

✍ HERE ARE SOME KEY THINGS I LEARNED ABOUT SYSTEMS

◊

◊

◊

◊

◊

◊

◊

◊

CHAPTER 3 – REVIEW QUESTIONS

1. Examine the idea of interdependence in the workplace: what it is, how it works, and why it matters.

2. Explain what we mean by 'systems thinking.' Why is it important in the workplace? Use examples.

3. Explore the two key questions to ask about interrelationships in a system. Why is it important to ask them together?

4. Explore the similarities and differences between systems thinking and griping. Use examples.

5. Examine flow charts: what they are, what they do, how to make them, and how they help think things through.

6. Examine three general questions about possible causes which are helpful in cause-oriented problem solving.

7. Examine 'backwards chaining.' Use examples.

8. Examine 'fishbone diagrams,' using examples.

9. Examine three common mistakes we often make when dealing with information about a problem.

10. Examine 'distribution analysis' as a way of analyzing possible causes of a problem, using examples.

11. Examine Pareto charts. How do they help in cause-oriented problem solving?

12. Examine the cause-oriented problem solving strategy: what are the stages, how do they work, and why are they needed. Use examples.

CHAPTER 4

WHO'S IN CHARGE HERE ANYWAY?

Mindful Worker Competencies
Explored in Chapter 4

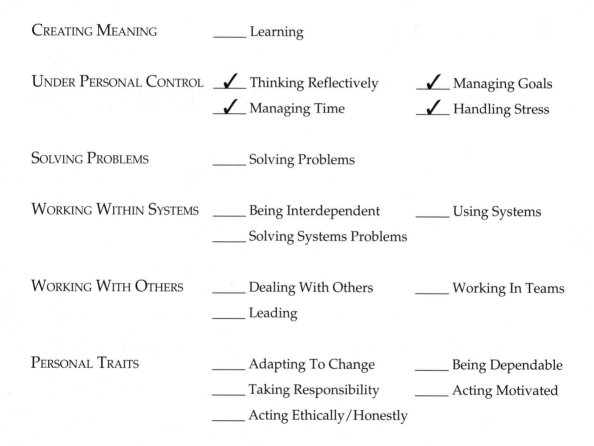

CREATING MEANING   _____ Learning

UNDER PERSONAL CONTROL   ✔ Thinking Reflectively   ✔ Managing Goals
                                       ✔ Managing Time   ✔ Handling Stress

SOLVING PROBLEMS   _____ Solving Problems

WORKING WITHIN SYSTEMS   _____ Being Interdependent   _____ Using Systems
                                         _____ Solving Systems Problems

WORKING WITH OTHERS   _____ Dealing With Others   _____ Working In Teams
                                         _____ Leading

PERSONAL TRAITS   _____ Adapting To Change   _____ Being Dependable
                                         _____ Taking Responsibility   _____ Acting Motivated
                                         _____ Acting Ethically/Honestly

Taking Your Mind Off Autopilot:
An Introduction

Airplanes have what is called 'autopilot': a device which automatically keeps the plane flying straight, level, in a certain direction, and at a certain speed. It's like a car's cruise control, except more complete.

Occasionally humans use autopilot also, don't we? How about driving to some familiar place, thinking deeply about something, and never really being conscious of the curves, speeds, and turns in the road. Our automatic mind has taken over from our conscious mind. Or how about when we're daydreaming in class, and suddenly become aware that we've unconsciously been taking notes?

Such physical or mental devices are valuable, but only when things are very predictable, unchanging, and in control. What would happen to an airplane which stayed on autopilot while flying straight into a thunderstorm, or a car which stayed on cruise control while approaching a red light? Messy.

The problem comes when we stay on mental autopilot while we are making decisions, facing changing situations, or taking new actions. The results are not usually as messy as broadsiding a truck at a red light, but they can be fairly painful. Over time, they can make our lives painful indeed.

How many times have you found yourself saying things like "I didn't think" or "I wish I had listened!" or "I wish I hadn't said that"? Most of us say that sort of thing to ourselves a lot. It's a sign that we've left our minds on autopilot when we shouldn't.

What do people really mean when they say things like: "You just don't think!" or "Give me employees who will think on their feet"? Basically, they are complaining *not* that the person can't think but that the person is not consciously and effectively using his or her mind; they are leaving their brains on autopilot. Their decisions and actions are thus weak.

This chapter is about getting your brain off of autopilot when that's useful. We will deal briefly with four different aspects of 'mental management':

◊ Being aware of and managing what you are **thinking**.

◊ Setting and achieving your **goals** and purposes.

◊ Managing your most precious resource: your **time**.

◊ Managing **stress**.

Just think what a mess you would be in if your mind automatically – with no conscious help from you – managed *all* of your thinking, purposes, time, and stress. You want your unconscious to handle *all* of these factors some of the time: that's healthy and wise. But *all* of the time? No way.

A final note. Each of these four areas could be a whole book or course in itself. What you're getting here is just a short introduction and overview.

Exercise 4A
METACOGNITION: GETTING IN TOUCH WITH OUR MINDS

Notice the first word of the title of this exercise. Metacognition. In the box below jot down your first reactions to that word.

✍ MY FIRST REACTIONS TO THE TERM 'METACOGNITION'

You might have written 'interesting' or 'new' or 'curious.' You were perhaps more likely to have written things like 'stupid' or 'scary word' or 'academic stuff.' You might have written 'yuck' or 'wow' or 'oh, no!' It doesn't matter what you wrote, because the key point is that you wrote *something*. By being aware of what your mind was thinking, you were in fact involved in metacognition.

A shorthand definition of metacognition might be something like "**awareness and management of what your mind is doing.**" If you were aware that your first mental reaction to the word was "Yuck. Nonsense," you were halfway there. If you were then aware of saying to yourself "I'd better not say that. The teacher probably takes it seriously," then you were into the second half of metacognition: consciously controlling the interactions between your mind and your actions.

Consider these two scenarios:

1 *Eric is trying to stuff a wad of papers into a small envelope. They won't go in. He moves them back out and shoves them in again. They still stick. After trying the same thing a third time, he shoves so hard that the envelope rips. Eric slams down the papers and walks away.*

2 *Lisa is trying to stuff a wad of papers into a small envelope. They won't go in. She moves them back out and shoves them in again. They still stick. She pulls them out, inspects the papers, and discovers that a paper clip is sticking to the back of the envelope, causing the problem. She moves the paperclip and inserts the papers smoothly into the envelope.*

All of us have had experiences like Lisa's and Eric's. We try to do something and it just doesn't work out right. If our minds are on autopilot, we act like Eric: react, repeat, and usually don't get anywhere positive. Sometimes, though, we act like Lisa. We move our mind into gear, think about what's happening, and solve the problem. Which one of these experiences involved metacognition?

There is really a lot to metacognition that lies below the surface of 'awareness and management.' We need to have some sense of our abilities, skills, weaknesses, styles, strategies, and the like. The more we are aware of these things, the more we can accurately weigh our situation and manage it in a useful fashion. But, for an introduction to the subject, let's just stick with 'awareness and management' at a relatively superficial level.

All of us have a constant mental conversation going on in our minds. Someone estimated that we 'talk to ourselves' at the rate of about 800 words per minute (try to talk that fast!). You heard yourself talking when you reacted to the word 'metacognition': you observed your mental conversation. Try it again now.

CLOSE YOUR EYES FOR TEN
SECONDS AND WATCH
WHAT YOU'RE THINKING.

Did you spot the following kinds of mental comments? "How can I watch myself think?" "Is ten seconds over yet?" "Closing my eyes feels funny," or "Wow, I'm doing it!" It's almost impossible not to think, and thinking involves your mental conversation. **Watching ourselves think seems strange not because it is unnatural but because it is unfamiliar.** You are not used to noticing what your muscles are doing (what are the muscles in your left leg doing right now?), but that doesn't mean that muscle action is unnatural. The same is true with our mind's actions; we just aren't used to consciously watching our mental conversation.

Here's another exercise to get you familiar with spotting your mind's inner workings. You will be read twelve words, each repeated twice. *After* you have heard all the words, and waited about 15 seconds, your job will be to write them down in the space below. The sequence doesn't matter. Just listen to the words, and then see how many of them you can write down. While doing this, watch your mind at work.

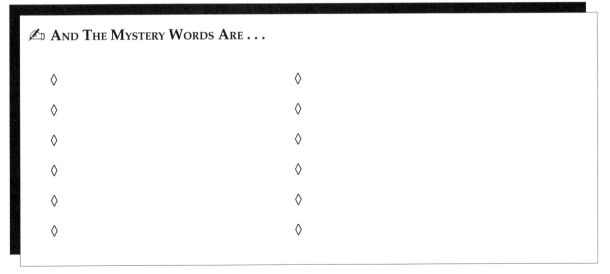

After you've checked your work, stop and 'check your mental processes.' Ask yourself what your mind was doing while you listened to those words. Share your insights.

Below are some lines out of a phone book. Use the information to do the tasks below. As you do each one, jot down what you were aware of your mind doing.

David, Elliott J.	942-3472	Davis, Paul & Maria	227-0204
Davis, Andrew Jr.	229-4810	Davis, Roberta	941-8853
Davis, Bill	941-2008	Davis, Sally & Jerry	223-1549
Davis, Diane	223-6857	Davis, William R. III	942-9840
Davis, Ed and Edna	229-3305	Dawes, Pamela R.	229-8734
Davis, Henry	942-4256	Day, Al and Gretchen	227-6859
Davis, Joe & Joanne	227-9873	Day, Arthur Camden	941-5656
Davis, K. F.	223-4820	Dennis, Dennis & Denise	223-2341
Davis, Magnolia	942-5563	Dennis, E. F.	229-3009

TASK 1

Find all of the people whose last name is Davis and whose first name starts with the letters H through P.

What was your mind doing?

✍

_____

_____

_____

TASK 2

Find all of the people whose telephone numbers begin with the numbers "223."

What was your mind doing?

✍

_____

_____

_____

_____

TASK 3

Find all of the people whose telephone book listing includes both the husband's and wife's name.

What was your mind doing?

✍

_____

_____

_____

Compare notes on what your mind was doing as you performed these three tasks. Compare the strategies that you used. Discuss what was hard and what was easy. Above all, talk about how clearly you were aware of what your mind was doing and whether or not you were telling yourself what to do next. By the way, did your metacognition kick in on the next-to-last names?

Although the idea of managing your mind may be a new concept for you, take comfort in the fact that there's 'method to the madness.' There is a general cycle which we go through as we watch ourselves think. That cycle has three simple parts that keep repeating in a spiral.

THE METACOGNITIVE CYCLE

STAGE 1: AWARENESS   "What's my mind up to right now?"

leads to ∇

STAGE 2: ASSESSMENT   "Is that an appropriate place to be?"

leads to ∇

STAGE 3: MANAGEMENT   "Leave it alone, or do something."

leads to ∇

STAGE 1: AWARENESS   "*Now* what's my mind up to? Did it work?"

Notice how natural this sequence is. It's like watching a machine start up or watching bacon fry. We observe and ask ourselves what's happening. Then we immediately make some kind of judgment. Then, based on our judgment, we either do something or let it go. Then we observe it again. And so forth. Imagine:

◊   **Watching an engine start up:**

∇ Awareness: "It's vibrating a lot."

∇ Assessment: "Should I shut it off?"

∇ Management: "Not yet. I'll wait and see what happens."

∇ Awareness: "It's still vibrating – maybe even a little more."

∇ Assessment: "It's gone on too long. It may be doing damage."

∇ Management: "I'll shut it down and check it out."

◊   **Watching bacon fry:**

∇ Awareness: "It's sizzling a lot."

∇ Assessment: "Is it sizzling too much? Is it too hot?"

∇ Management: "Don't think so. I'll let it go, but watch it."

∇ Awareness: "Now there's smoke coming up."

∇ Assessment: "That probably means it's starting to burn."

∇ Management: "I'll turn down the heat."

Notice that in both situations only the last stage involved physical action. All the rest of the 'action' was purely mental: your metacognitive conversation. Someone observing you might have judged that you were just standing there staring at something but not doing anything. In fact, you were doing a lot; it was just all mental action rather than physical action.

Now is your opportunity to imagine a mental conversation. Below are listed some other every-day events. For each one, write down an imaginary conversation you might be having as you were aware of and managing that event.

✍ CREATE A MENTAL CONVERSATION

On a separate sheet, write down two cycles of mental conversation for each situation, as on the previous page. Use your imagination to create them.

◊　Driving down a street trying to find a place you've never been.

◊　Watching an infant trying to take her first steps.

◊　Working a complex math problem.

◊　Reading a description of a technical procedure.

◊　Completing a short-answer question on a history test.

◊　Checking for flaws in items moving on a conveyer belt.

◊　Balancing a checkbook.

Now let's tap into someone else's conversation. Read the following mental conversation that Sherrie is having as she drives along. **Underline the metacognitive cycles she runs through in her mind.**

"There's Ben. Should I wave at him? That truck's close in front of me. Too close? Better slow down. Now I can decide whether or not to wave to Ben. He's gone, so it's too late. Goodness, that truck's smokey! Should I close the window? Too much trouble, and he's turning anyway. Oops. We've stopped at the light and he's sitting there ahead of me, belching smoke. Close the window? Can't take it any more, so I will. He's turning left. Do I have room to squeeze by him on the right? Will be narrow, but I'll give it a try. Oops, there's a cop. Would he ticket me for passing on the right? Better not take a chance. I'll sit here and wait . . ."

The first key to metacognition is awareness. We're not trained to be aware of our mind's functioning, and yet:

HOW CAN YOU BE IN CONTROL OF WHAT YOU'RE NOT AWARE OF?

Clearly, you can't. Things may work out well, but if so it will be because of luck, experience, or trained instinct. Most of us would rather get to our destination because the pilot was paying attention, not because of luck.

The only way to become more aware of your mind's functioning is to practice. Practice constantly, in class, driving home, at work, etc. Here's one more chance to practice in this text. Below is a half-page of information from a business article entitled "Metacognition: Don't Leave Home Without It" (Lee, Sept., 1989, Training magazine). On the right side is a space beside every line. Your task is to be aware of your thinking as you read this article by putting check marks in those spaces.

✍ **INSTRUCTIONS:** KEEP YOUR PEN BESIDE THE SPACES ON THE RIGHT. MAKE A CHECKMARK EVERY TIME YOU ARE AWARE OF YOUR MIND TRYING TO MAKE SENSE OF WHAT YOU ARE READING. JUST MAKE CHECKS, THEN KEEP READING.

Metacognition means being aware of your thinking processes. Morton Hunt described it this way: "Metacognition is . . . the monitoring and guiding of one's own thought processes; it is mind observing itself and correcting itself . . . It's thinking about the processes you use while you are learning . . . But metacognition also involves your ability to conclude, 'I don't understand that speaker's point. I'd better ask a question so that I do.' You've become aware that you will not reach your goal of gaining new knowledge unless you use another strategy to get there. Your metacognitive monitor has kicked in to aid in your comprehension."

Ruth Clark uses the computer as a metaphor for this function of human information processing. "Metacognition is like a computer's operating system," she says. "It monitors, controls, & manages the subordinate processes of encoding, acquiring, and connecting new information." Clark also applied the concept to an individual's ability to determine the goal of a task, apply the appropriate strategies to reach the goal, monitor progress toward the goal, and adjust strategies as necessary. "When an individual is performing a familiar task, these cognitive processes go on more or less 'mindlessly,' " she explained, "but when faced with a novel task or new problem, an individual with well-developed metacognitive skills consciously applies learning and problem-solving techniques."

Exercise 4B
GOALS: MANAGING WHERE YOU'RE GOING AND HOW TO GET THERE

"Goals" somehow sound like very heavy and serious things. It can't be much fun worrying about goals, can it? Yet how about these goals: having fun on a trip, getting an A with the least possible effort, feeling proud that you've done a good job, going to a concert (classic, rock, or otherwise), getting a good night's sleep, saving $100 towards something special, enjoying a quiet hour with a close friend. All of those are goals, even if short-term ones. And for most of us all of those are pleasurable rather than heavy and serious.

REALITY # 1
WE ALL HAVE GOALS

We have lots of goals. We change them all the time. And, like it or not, we spend a great deal of time and energy thinking about and trying to achieve our goals. Even the person whose goal is to do as little as possible in school and still get by will spend considerable time, or at least psychological energy, pursuing that goal. It's not easy to 'just get by.'

REALITY # 2
OFTEN OUR GOALS SEEM TO CONFLICT

Because we want so many things, some of them are bound to conflict. We want a good grade, but we also want to go out, spend time with our family, sleep, or whatever. We always seem to have to be choosing one thing or another! Seldom do we have a goal which is so isolated that we can pursue it without cutting back on or giving up something else.

REALITY # 3
GOALS AND DESIRE AREN'T THE SAME

Actually, though, we have more desires than we have goals. Goals are more hard edged, more specific, and often more long term. I might desire to sleep or go out right now, but my *goal* is to finish school, get a promotion, have a strong family, etc. My goal might be to comprehend a difficult text chapter, while my desire might be to get finished quickly. The key to eliminating some of the anxiety of choosing "this or that" is being clear on our more definite goals, then letting our desires fall into line.

REALITY # 4
UNCLEAR GOALS LEAD TO POOR RESULTS

Often our goals are not as clear as we might think; if pushed, it might be hard to say exactly how high a GPA is acceptable, or how rapidly we want to gain a promotion, or how much 'quality time with the family' is enough. Without that clarity, though, we will make mistakes which we could avoid. How does a working single parent in college balance her choices effectively? Only by being clear on how much GPA, promotion, or quality time to strive for. Amounts above the minimum can be traded off for other goals, if necessary. But, of course, those who have *no* idea what their goals are will be even less likely to end up where they want to go.

Being well-meaning or even attentive to what we're trying to do, however, is not always enough. The following situations, and endless other ones portray good people who got things messed up mainly because they were not clear on their goals.

◊ The new machine operator who diligently keeps the machine running until the moment when the motor burns out; he never knew he was supposed to keep it running *cool*, so it overheated while he watched.

◊ The student who busily memorizes a difficult medical procedure, but then when called upon is totally unable to *apply* it; not knowing that the purpose was application, she never ran through it visually, found ways to practice, etc.

◊ The father who leads his family through a very packed, fast-paced vacation, only to discover later that the rest of his family really wanted a slow-paced vacation where they could spend time enjoying a few places and things.

◊ The young child who, asked to 'pick some flowers from the garden,' returns with a large handful of flower petals but no stems.

You may not have noticed, but 'clarity of goals' is in fact a key part of everything we've already covered in this book. Think about how 'knowing your goal' is an important element in each of the following. Jot down your ideas. The first one is already filled in, as an example.

✎ How Does Knowing Your Goals Help With . . .

Metacognition ?

Awareness   our goals/purposes help define what we are aware *of* (e.g., machine speed, heat, sound, items produced, item quality, etc.)

Assessment   how do we know what 'good' is without goals?

Management   goals usually dictate our corrective actions & strategies

Solving Problems?

Using Systems?

Managing Time?

By now you should be getting the idea that being clear about your goals has an impact on very many important things in your life. What are some of your major goals?

✍ WHAT GOALS DO YOU HAVE?

List one of your school goals:

List one of your work goals:

List one other life goal:

Now that you have listed three goals, let's check out how clear they are. Below are some good criteria to use in evaluating your goals. Look at the three goals you've written and critique them. If that goal meets a criterion, put a "yes" or a checkmark in the appropriate line.

✍ THE WINDEX TEST: MEASURING THE CLARITY OF YOUR GOALS

SOME CRITERIA FOR CLEAR GOALS	LIFE GOAL	WORK GOAL	OTHER GOAL
1. Is it stated positively?	____	____	____
2. Is it realistic?	____	____	____
3. Will you know when you achieve it?	____	____	____
4. Are there 'landmarks' along the way (so you'll know how you are doing)?	____	____	____
5. Does it depend a lot on others?	____	____	____
6. Does it have a rough timetable?	____	____	____
7. Does it have a clear payoff?	____	____	____
8. Is it an *intrinsic* goal (something you want, not something others want)?	____	____	____
9. Is it more important than many/most of your other goals?	____	____	____
10. Does it make clear 'how much is enough' to satisfy you?	____	____	____

Probably the goals you wrote on the previous page did not meet all of these criteria. Pick one of your three goals and rewrite it below, making it as detailed as possible (to meet all or almost all of these criteria):

✍ **A REFINED GOAL:**

There are many aspects of goals that are important, but right now let's just stick with two of them.

GOALS

These are the outcomes you want to achieve, or the situation you want to bring about. They can be long-term (years), medium term (months), or short-term (days, hours).

ENABLING GOALS

Enabling goals are the things you must (or should) do first in order to accomplish your broader goals. You often need several of them to achieve a goal.

To figure out your enabling goals you often have to 'work backwards.' For example, think of a city about 50 miles away that you know how to get to. What's the closest town to that city on your route? To get to the city (goal) you first must get to that town (enabling goal). To get *there* you must first reach another town closer to you. And so forth, all the way back to where you are right now. It might look like this:

HERE $\longrightarrow$ town $\longrightarrow$ town $\longrightarrow$ town $\longrightarrow$ CITY

Shown that way, it looks kind of obvious and maybe stupid. We all know that you have to go through those towns first. BUT too often we fail to notice that the same thing is true with our more significant life goals. Consider this example:

HERE $\longrightarrow$???? $\longrightarrow$???? $\longrightarrow$???? $\longrightarrow$ JOB PROMOTION

Now it looks a little more sensible, doesn't it? You knew the names of the towns between you and that city, and the order in which you would have to get to them. But how about someone who is working and wants to get a promotion? What are *their* enabling goals: the places or achievements they must pass through in order to get to that goal? Here's a very brief guess at what the trip might look like.

> **In order to get the job promotion** I need to:
> ◊ *Be seen by my supervisor as being promotable.*
>
> **In order to be seen as promotable** I need to:
> ◊ *Perform well with additional responsibility.*
>
> **In order to perform well with additional responsibility** I need to:
> ◊ *Do a good job now.*

That's a very brief trip, of course, but it ends up like this:

| HERE | $\longrightarrow$ | Good Job Now | $\longrightarrow$ | Good With Additional Responsibility | $\longrightarrow$ | Seen As Promotable | $\longrightarrow$ | **JOB PROMOTION** |

Often our enabling goals don't fall into a linear sequence (accomplishing this . . . leads towards accomplishing that . . . leads towards accomplishing the other thing). For example, if my goal was to 'have a whole weekend free to visit out of town,' I might have one string of enabling goals relating to getting the kids taken care of, another relating to getting chores and tasks done ahead or put off, and a third relating to arranging for what I would do out of town. Those chains of enabling goals would all be needed, but they wouldn't necessarily relate to each other.

Now it's time to practice this idea of chains of enabling goals lying between us and our larger goals. Take one or more of the following goals and try to identify and organize as many enabling goals as possible for achieving that overall goal.

✍ IDENTIFY THE ENABLING GOALS FOR GETTING FROM HERE TO THERE

HERE	???????????????	A FINAL GPA OF 3.25 OR BETTER
HERE	???????????????	A WELL-PAYING ENTRY-LEVEL JOB IN MY FIELD
HERE	???????????????	BUYING A NEW CAR OF MY CHOICE
HERE	???????????????	HAVING TWO WEEKS FREE TO DO WHAT I WANT

✍ A FINAL TASK RELATED TO GOALS:

Select One Of The Goals You Identified Earlier And Lay Out The Enabling Goals You Need To Achieve It

Exercise 4C
TIME: MANAGING ONE OF YOUR MOST IMPORTANT RESOURCES

"Time is money," said the busy doctor. "Yes, but money is also time," replied the industrialist. What does this little by-play mean? The doctor rightly observes that her time translates into number of patients who can be seen, which translates partly into income. Squandering her time, in fact, loses her money.

The industrialist's reply? She reminds us that those with money can purchase a person's time, by hiring him or her. We can, in fact, view a salary as a payment for our time, plus the good works we can accomplish in that time.

All of us realize that money is one of our important resources. We tend to guard and use our money wisely. Yet, curiously, many of us tend to waste our time, to use it impulsively and unwisely. We do not regard our time as one of our most important resources.

If we do not see our time as a resource, maybe it's because we feel that we have enough of it. Those with this attitude feel that they can 'spend time' doing all the things they must or want to do, with some left over. They see themselves as rich in time (as opposed to rich in money, which few feel they have enough of).

Yet ask a person who is working, going to school, and raising a family or looking after aged parents. Ask someone who is working two jobs in order to support a family. Ask someone who has many community commitments in addition to work, family, etc. Ask someone whose job has expanded enormously, and who is trying to get three times as much done in the same amount of time. Such people will be much more aware of time as a precious resource. They will tend to manage it much more wisely, because they use it all.

Let's begin this exploration of managing your time by getting some sense of where you, personally, spend your time now. Think about an 'average' week, and in the spaces below list the hours you tend to spend on each function. There are blank spaces for you to add functions of your own.

✎ WHERE DO MY HOURS GO?

Hours/Week	Doing This:	Hours/Week	Doing This
_____	Sleeping	_____	Studying
_____	Eating	_____	With Family
_____	Driving/Going	_____	Recreation
_____	Work at a Job	_____	Work at Home
_____	In School	_____	
_____	Shopping	_____	

How did your time work out? Write the number of hours you accounted for in the first blank line in the equation below. Then complete the equation.

$$168 - \underline{\hspace{2cm}} = \underline{\hspace{2cm}}$$

What have you just calculated? Those of you with a positive number have calculated the number of hours per week that you cannot easily account for. Does that mean that this is wasted time? Not necessarily. BUT it's time you are not really in charge of – you don't know where it's going. It is missing in action.

Those of you with a negative number have just found yourself spending more time than you have available each week. That means two things. First, you need to reduce your estimates a bit. Second, you're probably in that group who are *very* aware of time as a precious resource – because you know you have so little of it.

No matter whether your number was positive or negative, you can probably benefit from becoming a little more in charge of your use of time. Those with a negative number can perhaps squeeze out a few more precious hours in the week. Those with a positive number can check to be sure that those 'missing in action' hours are being used to meet your own personal goals. Also, as your life becomes more complicated you can insure that you remain 'rich in time' by managing it.

Let's do a quick survey of some of your time-use patterns. Think back over the past week or month, then answer the following questions about your **general patterns** as realistically as you can. Check one blank for each question.

✐ Is This Mostly True Of Your Pattern?	Yes	No
1. I arrive on time.	——	——
2. I plan my week in advance.	——	——
3. I have trouble getting everything done.	——	——
4. I keep and use a large-sized monthly calendar.	——	——
5. I put off big assignments until the last minute.	——	——
6. I make lists of things I have to do.	——	——
7. I use my time between classes productively.	——	——
8. I don't manage to study until just before tests.	——	——
9. I get projects in late, or have to take shortcuts.	——	——
10. I plan out my work for the entire term at the start.	——	——
11. Projects and deadlines catch me by surprise.	——	——

Your answers to these questions may give some idea about your effectiveness in managing your time: for school, work, and your other lives. A sound time manager would have answered as follows: **yes** for questions 1, 2, 4, 6, 7, and 10, and **no** for questions 3, 5, 8, 9, and 11. You can use that pattern to make your own judgments. The question is: what can you do to improve your use of your time?

GRAVE ROBBERS OF TIME

"Grave robbers of time" sounds like a science fiction book. But the reality is that there are some very serious ('grave') habits or behaviors which rob most of us of a lot of our time. They account for much of the 'missing in action' time. Think about your hours, days, and weeks. Then, below, list as many grave robbers of time as you can. For each behavior you list, suggest a safeguard – something you might do to guard against that behavior. One example is given.

✍ GRAVE ROBBERS OF TIME

ROBBER # 1: GETTING SIDETRACKED

SAFEGUARD: Be aware of what your mind is doing (Remember metacognition earlier in this chapter?). Also, be clear on your goal.

ROBBER # 2:

SAFEGUARD:

ROBBER # 3:

SAFEGUARD:

ROBBER # 4:

SAFEGUARD:

ROBBER # 5:

SAFEGUARD:

You can make great strides in getting more control of your use of time by: being aware of the need, being conscious of your patterns, and safeguarding yourself against the grave robbers of time. There are, however, some other things that a student can do. Following are some suggestions of behaviors which lead to more efficient studying. Efficiency, in turn, saves you time for other things.

◊ Study in 1-3 hour chunks. Effective studying requires that you 'get into it' fairly deeply. You need time to get involved, immersed, and processing fully. BUT you also need periodic breaks, and your mind gets very inefficient after about 3 hours.

◊ Review just before and after class. Reviewing just before class gets your 'mental motor' running, while reviewing after class provides a very valuable second mental trace for what was covered in class that day.

◊ Review with 3x5 cards in spare moments. These are two tips for efficiency. First, jot key points down on 3x5 cards, and keep them with you. Then use your stray moments, 15 minutes or so, to review a few cards. Great for effective processing.

◊ Use written study plans. 'Planning to study history tonight' is a worthy intention, but it is favorite prey for the grave robbers of time. Things come up, and your plan goes down. It is far better to write out your plans in various forms: monthly calendars, weekly schedules, and daily to-do lists.

◊ Lay out a plan for long-term projects. Most long-term projects (such as reports, major papers, etc.) have to be done in stages. As soon as you get the assignment, break them into parts (hint: use the 'enabling goals' technique covered in the previous section). You will often discover that you need to take the first action now in order to get the others done well.

✍ TIME-PATTERN ITEMS. Remember the eleven time-pattern items you rated yourself on two pages ago? You probably interpreted them as school tasks. They are listed again below. **Check those that also apply to work.** Explore the implications.

_____ 1.   I arrive on time.

_____ 2.   I plan my week in advance.

_____ 3.   I have trouble getting everything done.

_____ 4.   I keep and use a large-sized monthly calendar.

_____ 5.   I put off big assignments until the last moment.

_____ 6.   I make lists of things I have to do.

_____ 7.   I use my time productively.

_____ 8.   I cram heavily for tests just before them.

_____ 9.   I get projects in late, or have to take shortcuts.

_____10.   I plan out my work for the entire term at the start.

_____11.   Projects and deadlines catch me by surprise.

Exercise 4D
STRESS: CONTROLLING THE CANNIBAL OF YOUR PERFORMANCE

Stress isn't necessarily a bad thing. It is simply our physical and mental reaction to changes in our environment. Since our environment is changing all the time, stress is a normal condition. The *problem* arises when we are under too much stress, for too long. Then stress does become a bad thing for us: it can 'eat us up' like some internal cannibal feasting on our minds and bodies.

HOW IS YOUR PERSONAL STRESS LEVEL? RATE YOURSELF ON EACH OF THE FOLLOWING BEHAVIORS.

I Do This:	Almost Always	Often	Some-times	Seldom	Almost Never
1. Know when I'm feeling stressed.	___	___	___	___	___
2. Walk away from decisions once I've made them.	___	___	___	___	___
3. See myself as competent to handle things well.	___	___	___	___	___
4. Can focus on one problem/task at a time.	___	___	___	___	___
5. Listen effectively in high-stakes situations.	___	___	___	___	___
6. Anticipate and combat negative thoughts about myself.	___	___	___	___	___
7. Am calm and patient when I have to wait.	___	___	___	___	___
8. Avoid 'going blank' when caught by a surprise request or task.	___	___	___	___	___
9. Approach tests, appraisals, etc., with confidence in the results.	___	___	___	___	___
10. Get adequate rest, nutrition, relaxation, and exercise.	___	___	___	___	___
11. Put past problems and mistakes behind me.	___	___	___	___	___
12. Carefully think through complex and/or emotional problems.	___	___	___	___	___

Your scores should give you some sense of how you are handling whatever stress you are under. The more checks you made in the left-hand columns ("Almost Always" and "Often"), the more you are likely to be handling your stresses well. If many of your checkmarks were to the right-hand side, you might think of whether or not your mental and physical performance are being diminished by stress. Bear in mind this is *not* a precise instrument; it at best, suggests some things for you to consider.

Let's look a little more deeply at this idea of stress as being normal and healthy unless it gets out of hand. Dr. Hans Selye, a scholar who spent decades trying to unravel the puzzle of stress, suggests that it can hit us at three levels of intensity.

THREE LEVELS OF STRESS INTENSITY

LEVEL 1 – ATTENTION

At this level, significant changes give us the 'butterflies.' They increase our alertness, our attention to detail, our willingness to get involved in adjusting to the change, and our motivation. We are responding to the change in a positive, flexible way: we are busy adjusting to it, or making it adjust to us.

LEVEL 2 – ANXIETY

At this level our emotions are getting more heavily involved. We may worry more and adapt less. We have either decided that a Level 1 response isn't doing the job, or we've been caught by surprise and gone directly to anxiety and fear. Our concentration is dropping, our mental ability suffering, and our cannibal is starting to get loose in our systems. Often we seem to have adapted, but hidden pressures remain and often grow unobserved.

LEVEL 3 – PANIC

In this stage we are no longer very functional. We have mental blocks (even to very simple information), we may stutter, etc. The internal pressures are so strong that our unconscious instinct to 'run away' is aroused. An important point: Level 3 stress can occur either suddenly through some surprise event or (more commonly) gradually, as internal, hidden stresses build up.

Does this sound confusing? Think of a small falling tree leaning against an electric wire. At initial contact the wire bends, adjusting to the tree: Level 1 accommodation. But then as the tree presses more heavily against it, the wire's supports creak with strain. Then, silence and apparent lack of motion. Nothing appears to be happening. Yet the tree is steadily shoving against the wire, stressing it and stressing it: Level 2. Finally this hidden stress becomes too great and the wire snaps: Level 3 is reached. Attention, anxiety, and then panic. Healthy, harmful, and then dangerous.

What causes such stresses in our lives? Lots of routine human events and reactions can cause or contribute to anxiety and panic. Consider these:

1. **Daily nuisances and irritants** can contribute to stress, if we let them.

2. **Relationships** can be a prime source of strength, and/or stress.

3. **Lack of or difficult goals** can be stressful, as we either feel ourselves to be aimless or are frustrated at seeing ourselves fall short.

4. **Beliefs and thoughts** can be stressful when conflicting with the realities we find around us in our jobs, at school, at home, etc.

There are, however, more major contributors to Level 2 and 3 stress. These tend to strike us not with the subtlety of patient pressure but with the blows of a sledgehammer. What are some of these sledgehammers? Listed below are twenty events which occur in many people's lives. All of them tend to cause major stress. Examine them, and then try to put them into four groups according to *how much* stress they cause: top quarter, second quarter, third quarter, and bottom quarter of the group of twenty. Put the letters for five causes in each group.

✍ MAJOR CAUSES OF SUDDEN STRESS

- a. Increasing arguments between parents and children.
- b. Family member arrested.
- c. Family member dies.
- d. Major problem at work.
- e. Child care arrangements collapse.
- f. Difficult or unwanted pregnancy.
- g. Family member becomes disabled or permanently ill.
- h. Parents become separated or divorced.
- i. Family purchases a new house.
- j. Family member becomes dependent on drugs or alcohol.
- k. Family member changes job or career.
- l. Family member marries.
- m. Increasing arguments between husband and wife.
- n. Family debts require a major new loan.
- o. Drug dealers move into neighborhood in force.
- p. Parent retires from work.
- q. Family member runs away from home.
- r. Aged parents move in with family.
- s. Parent loses job.
- t. Close family friend dies.

TOP FIVE	SECOND FIVE	THIRD FIVE	BOTTOM FIVE

Often the everyday 'pinprick' types of stresses combine with the 'sledgehammer' types to create major stress. Worry about an aged parent's lingering illness, for example, can mutate over time as the concern over their condition becomes partly overshadowed by the daily grind of visits, chores, loss of sleep, need for patience, etc.. At such times the pinprick irritants which can usually be tossed aside with ease are somehow harder to ignore. They bite deeper and the itch lasts longer. This makes the larger problem greater, and thus the stress grows deeper. Often, however, that stress is hidden beneath a feeling of numbness. Or maybe we pretend that the stresses caused by the parent's illness 'really aren't there.' We tell ourselves that we shouldn't be stressed if we truly loved our parents. Thus we slip through Level 2 anxiety towards Level 3 panic.

Symptoms Of Stress

Because we can move from one stress level into the next so silently and often unconsciously, it is important to be able to gauge our stress level from time to time (and frequently when we know we're under stress). How do you do that? Whether you're a worker or a student, you might want to watch yourself (remember metacognition?) for certain symptoms. Here are several; see if you can list some others based on your own experience.

Symptom: *Unable to concentrate.*
Symptom: *Regularly feeling discouraged.*
Symptom: *Preoccupation with the negative.*

✍ Symptom:

✍ Symptom:

✍ Symptom:

✍ Symptom:

✍ **When We See These Symptoms In Ourselves, Why Is It Hard To Talk Ourselves Out Of Feeling Stressed?**

Strategies For Coping With Undue Stress

The key question is: what can we *do* about stress when it's threatening to get out of hand? No single strategy works for everyone. In fact, most of the time we need to pick two or three strategies to use in combination. Why is that? No one strategy can work all the time, and the first moment it isn't working we tend to get all stressed again by the fact that it isn't working. But if we use more than 2-3 strategies, then we most likely will not use any of them very long. Here are some strategies which often work in reducing stress.

Set Realistic Goals

Frequently as we realize we're under stress we set huge goals for ourselves ("I'm going to be always loving to my father with Alzheimer's who lives with us"). Most of us can't reach them. And failure to do so just creates more stress in us. Instead, set small, reachable goals; see the previous section on goals for reminders of how to do this.

Burn Out The Tension

When under stress we often feel physical tension: the shakes, clenched fists, shrill voice, etc. An oddly useful stress-release technique: carry the physical signs to the extreme and burn them out. Shake hard. Clench fists until they ache. Talk highly, rapidly, and shrilly (in private, of course). Overdo the physical sign until it burns out, and takes stress with it.

Make Some Victories

Often, people who are over-stressed may feel defeated. As they move through Level 2 anxiety, they do in fact perform less well, adding to their sense that things have gotten the better of them. They doubt their ability to succeed. They very much need a victory . . . *any* victory. A very useful strategy is thus to find something very tangible to reduce stress and accomplish it: one less cigarette, don't yell at the kids for the next 5 minutes, etc.

Separate Feelings From Thoughts

Many of our stressful thoughts are not, in fact, thoughts. They are feelings. When we say, "I *wish* he'd give me just a few minutes of peace," what are we really saying? We're saying that we feel: tired, frustrated, angry, scared, hopeless, etc. Seeing underneath our words and apparent thoughts to the hidden feelings can help a lot. By recognizing the feelings, we can begin to accept them as just part of ourselves. More importantly, we can move towards accepting ourselves.

Accept Ourselves

Often we increase our stress by blaming ourselves for *being* stressed: "I should *want* to care for him!" We can begin reducing stress by not blaming ourselves for the fact that we *are* under stress. Being under a lot of stress is more of a situation than a character flaw. Even if we are prone to stress, it doesn't help to whip ourselves. Accept the fact and then move on.

Picture A Stop Sign!

One of the best ways to temporarily halt a stress attack is to visualize a stop sign. Sound crazy? Remember the earlier discussion of 'limited capacity information processors'? See if you can recall the image of seven items of thought crowded into a room with hundreds of other thoughts outside, clamoring to get in. Now, what if most of those seven items are stress-thoughts and all you can do is think about *them*? No others will be allowed in. The stress thoughts refuse to leave, and until they do there's no way you can get unstressed!

Unless you can push those stress thoughts out. That's where a stop sign comes in. You probably can't push them out with rational thinking. But tell yourself to imagine a big, red stop sign. Visualize the color. The shape. The size. The letters. Guess what? Your active mind is now filled with a stop sign. The stress thoughts have left. You can now *choose* what thoughts to let in when the stop sign leaves. If you're smart, you won't choose to let the stress thoughts in again.

✍ Some Ways I Can Reduce My Stress . . .

Suggest two other stress-reduction strategies that sometimes work for you.

1.

2.

Exercise 4E
TAKING CHARGE: MAKING YOUR MAP

This chapter contained four different mindful worker competencies. As you have done in the previous chapters, help develop the profiles of people who are exceptional, and then rate your current status and your goals, in each of these areas:

◊ Thinking Reflectively.
◊ Managing Goals.
◊ Managing Time.
◊ Managing Stress.

✍ PROFILE OF AN EXCEPTIONAL REFLECTIVE THINKER: Someone who feels their 'wheels turning' when faced with something to think about. Who can be aware of what their mind is doing. Someone who can change direction if necessary.

Someone who:

Someone who:

✍ RATE YOUR OWN REFLECTIVE THINKING COMPETENCE

HORRIBLE				FAIR					EXCELLENT
1	2	3	4	5	6	7	8	9	10

"X" point = current status   "Circle" point = 2-3 year goal

✍ WAYS TO *IMPROVE* YOUR COMPETENCE:

✍ WAYS TO *PROVE* YOUR COMPETENCE:

✍ PROFILE OF SOMEONE WHO IS EXCEPTIONAL AT MANAGING GOALS: Someone who knows what they want and how to get it. Who can sort out their priorities. Who can identify the main steps they need to take in order to accomplish something.

Someone who:

Someone who:

✍ RATE YOUR OWN COMPETENCE AT MANAGING GOALS

HORRIBLE				FAIR					EXCELLENT
1	2	3	4	5	6	7	8	9	10

"X" point = current status   "Circle" point = 2-3 year goal

✍ WAYS TO *IMPROVE* YOUR COMPETENCE:

✍ WAYS TO *PROVE* YOUR COMPETENCE:

✍ PROFILE OF SOMEONE WHO IS EXCEPTIONAL AT MANAGING TIME: Someone who is very organized in terms of knowing what they will do when. Who gets a lot done in a short time. Someone who keeps and uses to-do lists.

Someone who:

Someone who:

✍ RATE YOUR OWN COMPETENCE AT MANAGING TIME

HORRIBLE				FAIR					EXCELLENT
1	2	3	4	5	6	7	8	9	10

"X" point = current status   "Circle" point = 2-3 year goal

✍ WAYS TO *IMPROVE* YOUR COMPETENCE:

✍ WAYS TO *PROVE* YOUR COMPETENCE:

✍ PROFILE OF SOMEONE WHO IS EXCEPTIONAL AT HANDLING STRESS: Someone who reacts calmly to sudden emergencies. Who can be thoughtful when surprise problems emerge. Who does not 'come unglued' when many things need to be done at once.

Someone who:

Someone who:

✍ RATE YOUR OWN COMPETENCE AT HANDLING STRESS

HORRIBLE				FAIR				EXCELLENT
1	2	3	4	5	6	7	8	9	10

"X" point = current status   "Circle" point = 2-3 year goal

✍ WAYS TO *IMPROVE* YOUR COMPETENCE:

✍ WAYS TO *PROVE* YOUR COMPETENCE:

Summary Of Chapter 4
TAKING YOUR MIND OFF AUTOPILOT

This chapter was rich in material about getting control of your life in five important areas: thinking, goals, time, concentration, and stress. Sort through some of your memories from the chapter and write down at least ten major points which you want to store actively in your long-term memory.

✍ HERE ARE SOME KEY THINGS I LEARNED ABOUT SELF-MANAGEMENT

◊

◊

◊

◊

◊

◊

◊

◊

◊

◊

◊

CHAPTER 4 – REVIEW QUESTIONS

1. Explain the meaning and roles of 'metacognition.'

2. Why is metacognition important to a mindful worker?

3. Discuss the metacognitive cycle: what it is, how the stages relate, and why it is important.

4. Discuss the criteria for clear goals: what they are, how they work, and why they are important.

5. Explain and give examples of the idea of 'enabling goals.'

6. Explain why the ability to manage your time is important in the workplace. Give examples.

7. Explain your own habitual pattern for managing your time. Discuss its strengths and weaknesses.

8. List and describe four grave robbers of time which especially apply to you. What can you do to combat them?

9. Discuss and give five examples of five symptoms of stress.

10. Examine the three levels of stress intensity: what they are, what they mean, how they relate to each other, and what they mean for the mindful worker.

11. Discuss strategies for coping with stress: what they are and why and how they work.

12. Be prepared to discuss the relationship of any one of the mindful worker competencies of this chapter to the other competencies we have covered, including problem solving, interdependence, and systems thinking.

CHAPTER 5

WHO ARE THESE PEOPLE AND WHAT DO THEY WANT?

MINDFUL WORKER COMPETENCIES
EXPLORED IN CHAPTER 5

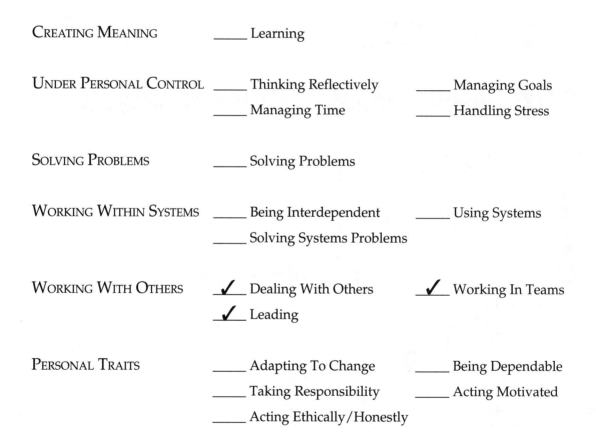

CREATING MEANING   _____ Learning

UNDER PERSONAL CONTROL _____ Thinking Reflectively   _____ Managing Goals
                        _____ Managing Time   _____ Handling Stress

SOLVING PROBLEMS   _____ Solving Problems

WORKING WITHIN SYSTEMS _____ Being Interdependent   _____ Using Systems
                        _____ Solving Systems Problems

WORKING WITH OTHERS   ✓ Dealing With Others   ✓ Working In Teams
                        ✓ Leading

PERSONAL TRAITS   _____ Adapting To Change   _____ Being Dependable
                        _____ Taking Responsibility   _____ Acting Motivated
                        _____ Acting Ethically/Honestly

Exercise 5A
WORKING WITH OTHERS, INDIVIDUALLY

People will be working more closely together in both the workplace and the schoolhouse in the 21st century. This trend is visible in many of the major change-oriented movements in both arenas: consumer orientation, the quality movement, collaborative learning, workplace problem-solving teams, and the like. This chapter briefly examines three aspects of that dynamics: dealing with others as individuals, as members of a team, and as leaders. All will be crucial roles for the mindful worker into the next century.

We will begin by exploring our dealings with others as individuals, which is the baseline competence for the other two. Obviously this will only be a very brief look since the topic of effective interpersonal relations occupies many feet of shelves in most libraries. It is a highly complex topic.

Interpersonal relations means the processes by which people deal with each other. That part is easy to say. The next part, however, gets a little more tricky. Try this question:

✍ **WHAT DO WE MEAN BY *EFFECTIVE* INTERPERSONAL RELATIONS?**

"Effectiveness" is a slippery word, isn't it? It might imply that both people go away happy, or that one person successfully convinces the other of something, or that the two people together accomplish some task or project. It might mean many things. Why? Because *effective* needs to be interpreted in terms of your *goals* (remember Chapter 4!). Within that context, is it safe to suggest that effective interpersonal relations means that both parties have their goals met? Or is it better to mean that both parties feel satisfied with whatever has taken place, even if both don't get their goals met? Chew on those possibilities.

A related question is *why* is it important for the mindful worker to be skilled at interpersonal relations, other than as a generally good ability to have. Let's revisit a couple of topics we've already covered. Answer this question.

✍ **WHY IS EFFECTIVE INTERPERSONAL RELATIONS IMPORTANT IN *SYSTEMS THINKING*?**

Hope you quickly recognized that linking different parts of a system together almost always means linking people together. You work, learn, or act in one piece of a system, and others do the same in other pieces. When you want to investigate and improve the linkages between those pieces, you must work with those inhabiting the other parts. If you're not highly effective at talking and working with those other people, then your systems skills will be correspondingly weakened.

Here's a second example of the importance of effective interpersonal relations, based on another key topic you've already covered. Below are listed the twenty-four general success competencies we explored in Chapter 1, and have revisited several times in later Chapters. In the blank before each of them place a letter to show how greatly performance in that area depends on effective interpersonal relations. If you think there is no dependence, leave it blank.

✍ **How Dependent Are These Competencies On Effective Interpersonal Relations?**

V = Very	S = Some	L = Little

___ Adapting to change	___ Taking risks
___ Listening	___ Handling stress
___ Working in teams	___ Thinking reflectively
___ Solving problems	___ Reading effectively
___ Taking responsibility	___ Leading
___ Dealing with others	___ Persisting
___ Acting motivated	___ Managing goals
___ Calculating	___ Managing time
___ Communicating	___ Acting ethically
___ Concentrating	___ Acting confidently
___ Learning	___ Using systems
___ Being dependable	___ Being interdependent

"Effective interpersonal relations" probably scored fairly high in your ratings. There are several areas in which it is virtually impossible to have a mindful worker skill without also being skilled at interpersonal relations. You won't really be good at helping others, using systems, etc., without that ability.

Books on interpersonal relations are filled with tips and techniques for getting along well with others. But to identify many of the most important behaviors we really don't need to go beyond our own experience. Think of your own life, and answer the following question. One starter example is given.

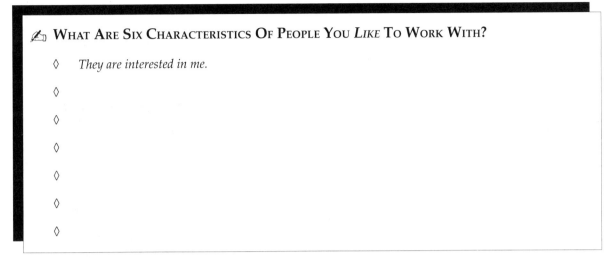

✍ **WHAT ARE SIX CHARACTERISTICS OF PEOPLE YOU *LIKE* TO WORK WITH?**

◊ *They are interested in me.*

◊

◊

◊

◊

◊

◊

You probably had more than six characteristics: we *know* what we like! And as you shared them with others you probably realized that your lists were very similar. Though we all have our individual styles and preferences, by-and-large the behaviors that please one of us tend to please most of us. That's the basis of effective interpersonal relations. Below, see if you can clarify some other things about effective human relations by looking at the negative side.

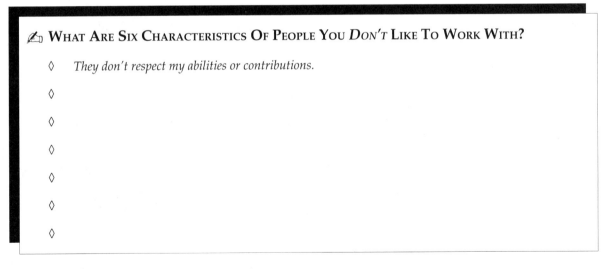

✍ **WHAT ARE SIX CHARACTERISTICS OF PEOPLE YOU *DON'T* LIKE TO WORK WITH?**

◊ *They don't respect my abilities or contributions.*

◊

◊

◊

◊

◊

◊

Probably some of yours were the flip side of the positive characteristics, but perhaps there were some new traits. How similar were your characteristics to others' lists?

Interpersonal relations is really more than just how you work directly with another individual. Equally important is the *overall environment* in which you work, learn, or live. For example, is it easier to work well with others in a high-stress job or a low-stress job? How about in a job where the bosses respect the workforce versus one where they distrust the workforce? The environment plays a significant part in day-to-day interpersonal relations.

Obviously there are some parts of the environment that you may not have much control over: the nature of the work, the deadlines, etc. But the mindful worker *can* influence a surprising amount of the environment. See how many partly-controllable aspects you can think of which might affect interpersonal relations. List them below; a couple of examples are given.

✍ **WHAT ASPECTS OF THE ENVIRONMENT COULD THE MINDFUL WORKER PARTLY CONTROL TO IMPROVE INTERPERSONAL RELATIONS?**

◊   *The trust level among co-workers.*

◊   *An emphasis on solving problems rather than blaming others.*

◊

◊

◊

◊

◊

◊

◊

You have an influence over a surprising amount of the environment around you, don't you? Explore the implications by answering the following question.

✍ **HOW MUCH MORE OR LESS CONTROL DO YOU THINK THE MINDFUL WORKER WILL HAVE IN THE HIGH PERFORMANCE WORKPLACE THAN IN TRADITIONAL WORKPLACES? WHY?**

Are the dynamics of effective interpersonal relations the same at home, in school, in social situations, and at work? Not exactly, but they are similar. Again drawing on your own experience, work through this exercise. It occurs in three parts; take them in order.

STEP 1: Fill in the spaces on the left-hand part of the chart below. List several factors influencing interpersonal relations which are related to their actions, other's actions, and the tasks to be done. Examples are given; fill in two other factors for each.

✍ IMPORTANT FACTORS AFFECTING INTERPERSONAL RELATIONS

PEOPLE ARE MORE EFFECTIVE *AT WORK* WHEN:	AT SCHOOL	AT HOME	WITH FRIENDS
They Do This:			
◊ *Care about those they work with.*	—	—	—
◊	—	—	—
◊	—	—	—
Others Do This:			
◊ *Ask for and respect their ideas.*	—	—	—
◊	—	—	—
◊	—	—	—
The Task:			
◊ *Gives them opportunities to work with others.*	—	—	—
◊	—	—	—
◊	—	—	—

STEP 2: In the blanks on the right side, check off which of those work-oriented items are also true for school, home, and with friends.

STEP 3: Write an answer to the following question:

✍ *Using the insights from this exercise, what could I do to improve my interpersonal relations skills?*

Exercise 5B
TEAMS: WHAT'S IT ALL ABOUT?

Teams can mean many different things. The dictionary gives us an initial sense of how varied the idea of 'teams' can be. Notice these two different definitions of teams, given by the same dictionary:

◊ Team – a group of persons joined together in some action or contest.

◊ Team – two or more draft animals harnessed together.

The first definition implies that people are working together mostly on a volunteer basis, to carry out some task they feel is important. The second definition implies that people are 'harnessed together' by some outside force, to do something they may or may not care much about at all. Remember the differences between the traditional and the high performance workplace? One hired 'hands' and the other employed 'heads.'

Which of these team definitions would fit a traditional workplace? A high performance workplace?

We all have our own mental images of 'teams' – what they're like, how they work, and what they do. But you have probably never verbalized that image, even to yourself. All of our images involve people together, but how much more can we agree on? Let's find out. Start by answering the following questions.

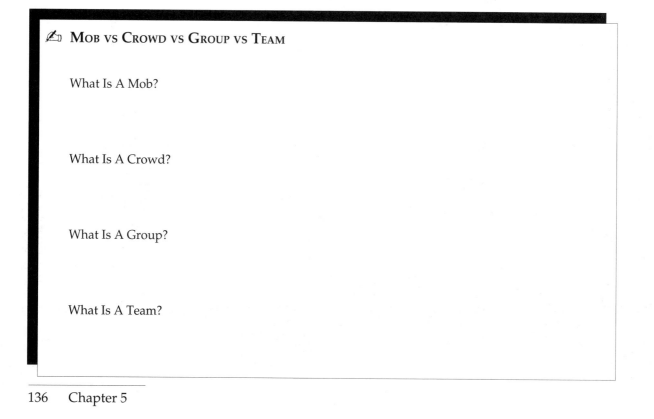

✍ MOB VS CROWD VS GROUP VS TEAM

What Is A Mob?

What Is A Crowd?

What Is A Group?

What Is A Team?

✍ Based on your previous definitions, what are the key distinctions between these terms? Check the following characteristics if they are important in distinguishing between such groupings of people:

___	Purpose?	___	Leadership?	___	Efficiency?
___	Size?	___	Use of talents?	___	Duration?
___	Organization?	___	Legitimacy?	___	Variety?
___	Other key characteristics?	(Specify:	_____	).	

It's not totally easy to distinguish between such terms, is it? Both crowds and teams may have purposes. Both mobs and groups can have leadership. A group and a team may continue for months or years. A riot mob would be illegitimate, but a mob running in fear from something would not really be illegitimate.

All of this is confusing. But surely you can put enough pieces together to play 'Beat the Dictionary!' Notice that a mob meets their first definition. You can do better than that. Below write a better definition of a 'team' than the one given you from the dictionary.

✍ **A NEW AND IMPROVED DEFINITION OF A TEAM IS:**

There are other aspects of teams that we must also worry about as we explore the dynamics of the mindful worker facing the 21st century. High performance workplaces make increasing uses of teams: teams working within a department, and teams cutting across departments. There are even teams that cut across companies! Yet teams can't do *all* the work, can they? Many times individuals have to do their own work, and make their own decisions.

BENEFITS AND DISADVANTAGES OF TEAMS

When are teams useful, and when are they not useful? At its simplest, teams (like any other process) are best used when their advantages outweigh their disadvantages. That's very obvious, isn't it? And not very helpful. To *make* that statement helpful let's look at the benefits and disadvantages of teams.

Below is the tale of Lackluster Video Rental Company. Lackluster has two problems: a short-term problem and a long-term problem. They are going to hire a 'team-building consultant' to help them solve both problems, and you are going to help the consultant. First read about Lackluster's sad story.

THE TEAMWORK SAGA OF THE LACKLUSTER VIDEO RENTAL COMPANY

BACKGROUND OF THE LACKLUSTER VIDEO COMPANY

Lackluster Video Rental Company runs a national chain of rental stores. It is an off-shoot of the Lackluster Buggy Whip & Horseshoe Company, and has been run in the same old traditional way as its parent company (which is now out of business). Lackluster Video's future looks pretty grim, also. Production has fallen as steadily as costs have risen. The workers are slack, angry, and uninterested. They used to be very alert, interested, and quality-oriented employees but now they don't seem to care if things are done right or not. The supervisors threaten, but nothing seems to work.

Now Lackluster has a real problem. Somehow, 50,000 special Madonna and Michael Jackson videotapes have been put into various cover boxes marked for Disney character children's videos. They've been shipped! And no one can find the records of which stores they have been sent to. Trouble is definitely brewing.

In desperation, Lackluster's top management realizes that things have to change. The mistake must be solved, but more importantly the workforce has to be recovered as a caring, committed, and helpful part of Lackluster's operation, if the company is to continue.

*Lackluster hires Sherlock Deming as a consultant. After investigation, Deming concludes that Lackluster must create teams of employees who are given authority to solve the short- and long-term problems. He observes that the line employees, rather than the top managers, **really** know what's going on and why the problems are occurring. They must be the ones to solve those problems, he argues.*

Lackluster's tradition-minded management doesn't like the idea. We know best, they say, just like our fathers who

ran Lackluster Buggy Whip and Horseshoe Co. knew best. Consultant Deming points out that their fathers are bankrupt, their company is gone, and the Lackluster Video Company is about to go under. If the Madonna-Mickey Mouse switch doesn't do them in, he argues, the next great goof by their indifferent 'hands' will surely do the job.

Consultant Deming shows Lackluster's management the chart comparing traditional with high performance workplaces (the same one you encountered in Chapter 1). He *points out that their **employees**, not their equipment, their money, or their long history, are Lackluster's most important resource. "Your employees can solve the problems if you all work together," he argues, "if you'll just free them up to work and think together, with each other and you."*

Frightened but desperate, Lackluster's management replies, "Tell us one more time of the long-term benefits of such teamwork. And show us again which of those benefits will also help us sort out the Madonna-Mickey Mouse problem before it hits the street."

Consultant Sherlock Deming, though frighteningly brilliant, is given to somewhat obscure and confusing speech. He becomes irritable if people such as the Lackluster managers ask him to be a little clearer. That's why he brings you along as his translator. It's your job to translate his comments into terms which his audience can easily understand.

Now's your chance to shine. Below are the many possible advantages of teams which Consultant Deming mentioned in his monologue. Use checkmarks to point out to Lackluster's top management which possible benefits are particularly important if you are creating: (a) a *long-term team* to solve Lackluster's basic production, quality, and cost problems or (b) a *short-term team* to deal with the Madonna-Mickey Mouse disaster (which you have about three weeks to solve). Don't worry about the final "S?" column right now.

✍ BENEFITS OF WORK TEAMS	LONG-TERM?	SHORT-TERM?	S?
1. Improve communications among units.	___	___	___
2. Get more people involved.	___	___	___
3. Sees various aspects of the problem.	___	___	___
4. Increases more people's sense of 'ownership' of the results.	___	___	___
5. Increases ideas and viewpoints.	___	___	___
6. Helps participants grow & develop.	___	___	___
7. Energizes things: more enthusiasm.	___	___	___
8. Taps more people's knowledge, experience.	___	___	___
9. Takes advantage of people's abilities.	___	___	___
10. Discovers hidden problems and needs.	___	___	___
11. Builds respect among those involved.	___	___	___

What does the Lackluster saga tell us? It helps us define the points at which teams help things out. But there are also disadvantages of teams. What are they? Some of them are listed below. Think and imagine, then add a couple of others.

✍ **DISADVANTAGES OF WORK TEAMS INCLUDE:**   S?

◊   Requires time and energy.   —

◊   May create friction, especially at first.   —

◊   May awaken hidden problems.   —

◊   Might lead to least controversial (but not best) solution.   —

◊   —

◊   —

◊   —

There's one final point to explore about the benefits and disadvantages of teams. You've noticed the curious "S?" in the last two exercise parts? Those stand for "School Teams." Go back and put a checkmark beside each benefit and disadvantage which apply to using learning teams in school. Then answer this question:

✍ **HOW DO THE BENEFITS/DISADVANTAGES OF TEAMS COMPARE AT WORK AND IN SCHOOL?**

Teamwork has many benefits for companies, yet for many years those benefits were not being realized, because teams were not used. Yet recently business dynamics have changed so that these benefits have become more important, even necessary. Teamwork also offers benefits to schools, yet like traditional businesses we are not taking wide advantage of those benefits. Think about this:

What pressures will make schools more inclined to use learning teams?

Exercise 5C
Teams: How Do They Do That?

Teamwork pays off, as you've seen, because teamwork is a key part of interdependence. But true teamwork is not an easy thing to develop. It requires a great deal of time, energy, and commitment on the part of the team members – and on the part of those creating the teams. In this exercise we will look briefly at several key parts of that transformation of groups into teams: roles, stages of evolution, and activities.

What Kind Of Team Do We Mean?

In the last exercise we noticed that the Lackluster Company had need of two different types of work teams: a short-term team to deal with the Madonna-Mickey Mouse problem, and a long-term team to improve operations and quality. For this exercise we will focus on the latter type of team: the group of people who work together over months or years to produce more cost-effective, quality products. Why do they work together like that? For pride and satisfaction, and so the company will be profitable and they will keep their jobs.

For this exercise, let's continue the saga of the Lackluster Video Company.

More From Lackluster Video

Consultant Deming (with your help) has convinced the top management of Lackluster Video Company to form its workforce into operational teams. Each team is made up of the workers in a particular production area, with the former supervisors working as an equal in the team (no longer the order-giver).

One new team is the Assembly Team. They run the area of production known as assembly. That area works like this. One production line makes the videotapes and sends them in endless streams down a conveyer belt. Another produc-tion line makes the cases and sends them down a separate conveyer belt. A third area makes labels and sends boxes of them to the assembly area.

All three functions come together in assembly. The videotape conveyer belt connects with the video case conveyer belt. Each videotape is supposed to slip smoothly into a case. Then a worker in the assembly area closes the case and slaps the correct label on it. Then the completed unit moves down another conveyer belt to the packaging area.

TEAM ROLES: WHAT DO THEY DO?

As we've explored, teams can't do everything: and shouldn't be asked to do so. What *should* they do? Let's find out what the Assembly Team should be doing. To do that, let's look at ways in which it is reasonable for one worker to help another out. Then you'll think about whether or not that is *also* something that the whole area team might help with.

Following is a list of things that one worker at Lackluster might do to help a fellow worker: on the left side. *First*, add some other things to the left-side list. *Then*, on the right side, suggest ways in which a team (consisting of the whole workforce in that area) might help out. Some examples are given.

✍ IDENTIFYING KEY TEAM ROLES AT LACKLUSTER VIDEO

WAYS ONE WORKER MIGHT HELP ANOTHER WORKER:		WAYS THE TEAM MIGHT HELP WITH THE SAME NEED:
◊ Be sure she had the proper tools and materials.	⟶	◊ *Assure quality supplies coming into assembly.*
◊ Help her out when overworked.	⟶	◊ *Schedule to avoid overwork.*
◊ Help her solve sudden problems.	⟶	◊ *Have a problem-solving system.*
◊ Help her improve her skills.		◊
◊ Share tips and knowledge with her.		◊
◊ Keep her updated on what's happening.		◊
◊ Help her feel she belongs.		◊
◊ Work to set common but reachable quality & production standards.		◊
◊ Making sure that Lackluster makes a profit (so everyone has a job).		◊
◊		◊
◊		◊
◊		◊
◊		◊

What you have really just done is to define many of the main tasks of a long-term work team (or what is commonly known as a 'self-managing work team'). They are a group of interdependent workers who cooperatively help each other (and other units of the plant) make the most cost-effective, quality product they can. That is their overall task as a team. Of course, this is only one type of team, but it is one of the most important for a mindful worker.

WORK TEAMS: HOW DO THEY EVOLVE?

Obviously Lackluster can't expect to take their current workers and instantly make them into an effective work team. Those workers have a lot of knowledge and skill and insight. They once had a lot of energy, enthusiasm, standards, and creativity. But they're used to working in isolation from each other, looking after themselves. They've gotten all of their orders from the supervisor, who has been doing the thinking for them (even when they didn't want that). They are not used to working as a team, using systems thinking, taking responsibility, and the like.

"What can we expect?" asked Lackluster's top management. Consultant Sherlock Deming responded that they should watch their workers go through four stages of evolution from their current situation to becoming a fully-effective team. Those stages are as follow:

> ### 4 STAGES OF TEAM EVOLUTION
>
> ◊   Stage 1 - Forming.
> ◊   Stage 2 - Storming.
> ◊   Stage 3 - Norming.
> ◊   Stage 4 - Performing.

These stages, Deming noted, involve not just activities but personal feelings among the team members. Below are the four predicted stages of team evolution. For each one, suggest some of the key feelings which the team members might anticipate.

> ### STAGE 1: FORMING

In this stage the team is organized and they begin to 'test the waters' – to see if it's really true, to figure out their boundaries, to explore roles and tasks.

In this stage team members might feel:

✍

_____

_____

_____

_____

_____

Stage 2: Storming

In this stage the team realizes its power, starts trying to do things, and runs into major problems. It lacks skills and experience, and everyone is trying to decide what their personal role is in the group. This is a tough stage.

In this stage team members might feel:

_____

_____

_____

_____

_____

_____

Stage 4: Performing

In this final stage the first three pay off. Minor achievements of the first three stages give way to major achievements, growing trust, increased skill at problem-solving, planning, and organizing, and a real sense of team identity.

In this stage team members might feel:

_____

_____

_____

_____

_____

_____

Stage 3: Norming

In this stage the team matures, accepts the difficulties along with the excitement, finds individual roles, builds trust, and most importantly, establishes the 'norms' (ground rules) by which the team can effectively operate.

In this stage team members might feel:

The top managers of Lackluster Video Company, by the way, have now formed themselves into their *own* team, with all its growing pains. As fears and anxieties are frequently soothed by Consultant Deming (ably assisted by you, of course), they move through perilous times of change. But at the end they, of course, find satisfaction and growing profitability as their team reaches stage 4.

Work Teams: How Do They Act?

By the time they reach the Performing stage, Lackluster's assembly team members have accomplished several things. They have changed their perception of their role and responsibilities as workers. They have learned to feel and act on trust and interdependence. They have gained many new skills and understandings. And, as a result of all that, they act very differently than they did in the Forming stage.

How do such teams act? Experts have prepared long lists of characteristics and behaviors of successful work teams. Most of those behaviors are common sense, such as:

◊ clear goals
◊ high standards
◊ practical groundrules
◊ defined roles
◊ clear communication
◊ collaborative climate

There are a few behaviors, however, that are particularly important to keep in mind as you participate in or observe effective work teams. Some are listed in the next column.

EFFECTIVE WORK TEAMS WILL, AS A GROUP:

◊ Work together
◊ Take responsibility
◊ Concentrate on tasks
◊ Help each other
◊ Take risks
◊ Persist at a task
◊ Act ethically
◊ Manage their time

◊ Solve problems
◊ Act dependably
◊ Listen well
◊ Use systems
◊ Be motivated
◊ Set clear goals
◊ Act confidently

Can you see how these behaviors would be very noticeable in the Lackluster assembly team as they reached the performing stage? These would be important contributors to their effectiveness as a team. Do you also notice something else about these behaviors?

✍ **WHERE DID YOU FIRST RUN ACROSS THE BEHAVIORS LISTED ABOVE?**

DO THE OTHER SUCCESS COMPETENCIES ALSO APPLY TO TEAMS?

There is much more that needs to be said about effective work teams, whether they are 'working' in businesses or in schools. But the most important thing to realize is that, for the high-performance firms that will thrive into the 21st century, effective work teams are as important as mindful workers. In fact, the reasons for both, and the competencies needed by both, are very much the same. What might we call groups of mindful workers? Mindful work teams.

Exercise 5D
Lead, Follow, Or Get Out Of The Way

Leadership, like teamwork, is a tricky concept to define clearly. Leadership obviously involves one person stimulating others to do a particular thing. But beyond that generality it is difficult to pinpoint exactly what leadership consists of. In fact, leadership is almost certainly *not* a single thing; it is many things. To understand leadership we need to ask questions about leading who, to do what, for what purpose, under what circumstances.

What Is A Leader, Anyway?

Let's start our exploration of leadership in much the same way as we did with the idea of a team. In the box below are a set of terms often related to leadership. Write down what you think of when you hear each of these terms.

✍ What's In A Word?

WHAT IS A MANAGER?

WHAT IS A SUPERVISOR?

WHAT IS A RULER?

WHAT IS A GUIDE?

WHAT IS A LEADER?

All of those types of people could be leaders in a certain fashion, couldn't they? We can lead by directing, by organizing, by commanding, by showing the way, and so forth. On the other hand, any of them can be something other than a leader. Many 'rulers' have worn crowns without being able to lead much of anything, at least in the sense that most of us understand leadership.

Let's try to get some sense of what we mean by "leadership" by answering the following questions:

If you have power over someone, are you their leader?

✍ _____

Do good leaders always have to have a goal in mind?

✍ _____

Do good leaders always have to be 'out in front'?

✍ _____

Are leaders in one situation leaders in another?

✍ _____

Are leaders always popular?

✍ _____

So, where are we now with the idea of leadership? We are ultimately back to very simple dynamics, and results. A leader has a goal in mind, and other people end up helping to achieve that goal. The dictionary defines a leader as, "**Someone who influences others to work towards a specific goal.**"

Can you improve on that definition of a leader?

✍ _____

What Does A Leader Do?

We can be a little more specific about the *roles* of a leader than we can about the definition of a leader. Let's draw on your own experience. Following are some typical community roles: we know (or know of)

people who have these positions. Think of some ways in which they might behave as a leader, and complete the statements. Some examples are given; add two more to each type.

✍ A Leader Is Someone Who . . .

A *businesswoman* would be a leader if she:

◊ *Changed her company from traditional to team-based operations.*

◊

◊

A *plumber* would be a leader if he:

◊ *Worked with a group to create a local special Olympics.*

◊

◊

A *student* would be a leader if he:

◊ *Spoke out against crime in the local community.*

◊

◊

A *teacher* would be a leader if she:

◊ *Encouraged a student arts council to form.*

◊

◊

Leaders can act in many different ways, can't they? Did you notice the title of this exercise, 'Lead, follow, or get out of the way'? It is often spoken or written as a frustrated warning to officials and managers who are not 'moving out' fast enough. But, in fact, it itemizes *three different ways to lead*. Think about your own experiences, and see if they don't support this interpretation. Read the following explanations, then see if you can add an example of your own.

LEADERS CAN BE 'OUT IN FRONT'

This is what we most often think of as the proper leadership position. Such leadership issues statements, calls for action, leads the charge, and so forth.

A personal example of such leadership is:

✍ _____

_____

_____

_____

_____

LEADERS CAN FOLLOW

This sounds strange, but it's true. Back in the 1960's a United States Congressman named Charles L. Weltner voted for the first major civil rights bill. He 'followed' the party line and also his conscience. He was the only Southerner to vote for that bill. Was he not a leader, though he chose to follow the leadership of others?

A personal example of such leadership is:

✍ _____

_____

_____

LEADERS CAN GET OUT OF THE WAY

It often takes great courage and leadership to 'get out of the way' of others' actions and events. For example, a company official, when told that her son was part of a group of students filing suit against her company for pollution replies, "I won't stand in his way. He believes in what he is doing." A leader?

A personal example of such leadership is:

✍ _____

_____

_____

_____

Have You Seen Them?

Which Way Did They Go?

I Must Find Them.

For I Am Their Leader!

Below are some of the many roles which leaders might play (whether they are leading, following, or getting out of the way). On the right side are a variety of circumstances: leader of a team or of individuals; leader in a traditional or a high-performance workplace; leader in school or in social situations.

YOUR TASK: Take each of the roles on the left, one at a time. Put a check if you think that a type of leadership role is *important* in each particular situation on the right. Do all of the roles.

✍ LEADERSHIP: WHAT AND WHEN?

THESE ARE LEADERSHIP ROLES:

ARE THEY IMPORTANT WHEN LEADING....

	Individuals	Teams	Trad'l	Hi-Perf. Workplaces	School	Social
1. Being a spokesperson.	__	__	__	__	__	__
2. Being a catalyst (causing things to happen).	__	__	__	__	__	__
3. Being a director.	__	__	__	__	__	__
4. Being a coach.	__	__	__	__	__	__
5. Being a cheerleader.	__	__	__	__	__	__
6. Being a salesman.	__	__	__	__	__	__
7. Being a servant (helping others lead & grow).	__	__	__	__	__	__
8. Being a devil's advocate (raising tough questions).	__	__	__	__	__	__
9. Being a facilitator (making things easier).	__	__	__	__	__	__

Your ratings underscore why it's hard to find a simple definition of leadership. Leaders can play so many different roles in so many different situations. Let's leave this exploration of leadership definitions and roles with one final topic: how do *you* fit in?

On the chart above, *circle* the numbers of the *three* leadership roles on the left that you are best at. Then *star* a fourth role: the one you want most to work on.

Exercise 5E
LEADERSHIP: HOW DO THEY DO THAT?

We tend to think of a movie star, a professional basketball player, and a surgeon as being highly skilled. They have natural talents, but then they have added many other skills and much knowledge through learning and practice. On the other hand, we often tend to think of a leader as being 'born, not made' – something that just happens.

That's not the case. Often people will show leadership traits at an early age. But then most of them become increasingly effective as they study, learn, and practice the skills of leadership. Yet there's a problem here. We can figure out where many movie stars, professional athletes, and surgeons develop their skills: they go to special schools and have special trainers. But how do leaders learn *their* skills of leadership? See if you can answer that from your own experience.

✍ **WHERE AND HOW DO LEADERS LEARN THEIR SKILLS?**

Though many companies, government agencies, schools, and the like now offer special leadership training programs, people aren't usually sent to them until they have *already* demonstrated considerable leadership skill. Where do they get it? Mainly from models and their own minds. They watch people who are leaders, notice what they are doing, and try to imitate the actions. They may question leaders about how they do this or that.

Often, leaders 'play out' situations in their minds, think about what might happen, and select a behavior according to the mental results. Even more frequently, they do things and notice the actual results. They then think through what went wrong and right, try to figure out why, and change their behavior accordingly. Most new leaders develop their basic leadership skills on their own.

CHARACTERISTICS OF A LEADER

We can identify many of the important characteristics of a leader by drawing on our own experience. Think of someone you consider a leader: nationally, locally, or in your own group. Think of how they *behave* when they are leading — what do they *do or exhibit* that makes them a leader in your eyes? List some of those leadership characteristics below.

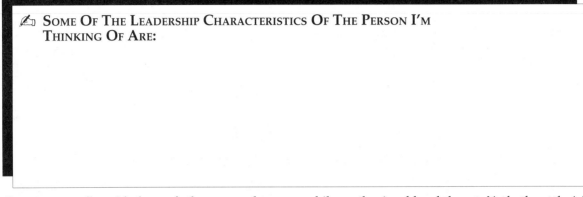

✎ SOME OF THE LEADERSHIP CHARACTERISTICS OF THE PERSON I'M THINKING OF ARE:

Compare your list with those of others around you. You will probably discover that you listed some of the same characteristics (even if differently-worded), and that some of the ones they listed fit your person also. But you will also find differences: traits they found that your person does not exhibit. Again, leadership is a very tricky and individual matter. For example, one leader can be extremely outgoing and friendly, while another is cold and abrupt. Yet both get the job done.

Following is a list of some leadership characteristics commonly found in research on leadership. See how they compare with the characteristics you listed. There is space to add a few more if you wish.

SOME CHARACTERISTICS OF A LEADER

a.	High energy level	l.	Handles conflict
b.	Listen well	m.	Creates trust
c.	Confident	n.	Good judgement
d.	Well organized	o.	Remains calm
e.	High morals/ethics	p.	Persuasive
f.	Builds consensus	q.	Respects others
g.	Clear goals	r.	Encourages others
h.	Knowledgeable	s.	✎
i.	Speaks well	t.	✎
j.	Dependable	u.	✎
k.	Develops others		

In the previous exercise you explored the many different roles that a leader can play: spokesperson, director, catalyst, coach, cheerleader, etc. You compared roles in six different situations. Following are those same six situations. **For each situation, identify (by letter) no more than eight of the leadership characteristics on the prior page which you think are especially important.**

✎ WHAT ARE THE MOST IMPORTANT LEADERSHIP CHARACTERISTICS

When leading a group of individuals?

When leading a team?

When leading in a traditional workplace?

When leading in a high-performance workplace?

When leading in school situations?

When leading in social situations?

After exploring the similarities and differences among the importance of these characteristics, answer this final question about important leadership characteristics.

✎ WHICH LEADERSHIP TRAITS SEEMED TO BE THE MOST IMPORTANT?

LEADERSHIP STYLES: THEORY X VS THEORY Y

There has been much discussion of what are known as Theory X and Theory Y management/leadership styles. To find out what they are (and where you fit in), answer the following questions. **Check whether you think each statement is Mainly True or Mainly False.**

✍ WHAT DO YOU BELIEVE ABOUT PEOPLE AND WORK?

MAINLY TRUE	MAINLY FALSE	STATEMENTS:
___	___	1. People will avoid work if at all possible.
___	___	2. People will accept responsibility if given a chance.
___	___	3. People will work hard for things they are interested in.
___	___	4. People prefer to be directed & supervised.
___	___	5. Working is as natural an instinct as playing.
___	___	6. People seek security and fear taking risks.
___	___	7. People are creative and flexible at work.
___	___	8. People must be forced to work hard.
___	___	9. People want to feel fulfilled and respected.
___	___	10. People prefer to avoid responsibility.

The above questions are really about human motivation; what do people want and need? The Theory X style is based on a fairly skeptical view of human motivation, while the Theory Y style is based on a fairly optimistic view.

There is no absolute "right/wrong" answer as to which theory is correct, since there are plenty of examples of both types of behavior. But the difference does play a major role in determining how people can best manage and lead in the workplace. A Theory X manager/leader, for example, will tend to be very directive and suspicious of his workforce; he will believe that they need to be strongly managed if they are to work well. The Theory Y manager/leader, on the other hand, will be more democratic and authority-sharing in relating to the workforce, whom he trusts to do their jobs well if given a chance.

How did you rate on the Theory X/Theory Y scale? Look at your responses, and indicate below where your answers fell.

◊ Theory X styles *agree* with Items 1, 4, 6, 8, & 10. Your score: ____.

◊ Theory Y styles *agree* with Items 2, 3, 5, 7, & 9. Your score: ____.

What do you think about those results? Do they fit your general beliefs about what motivates people in the workplace? It's important to know what you believe about people's motivation if you plan to be a leader, because that will have a major impact on your leadership style. It will also impact the kind of organization you choose to be a part of: traditional or high-performance.

Which Theory Fits Best With High-Performance Workplaces?

Theory X? ____   Theory Y? ____

Few leaders, of course, are *totally* Theory X or Theory Y in their behavior. Normally they are somewhere in between, though tending towards one set of beliefs or the other. One way to look at the practical implications of these differences is to look at a range of leadership styles. This range means that something is a little bit at one extreme, and total at the other extreme. To better understand what that means, look at this graph.

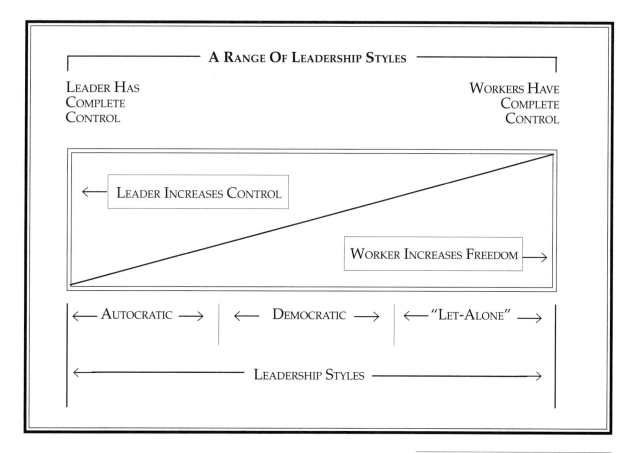

A RANGE OF LEADERSHIP STYLES

LEADER HAS COMPLETE CONTROL

WORKERS HAVE COMPLETE CONTROL

← LEADER INCREASES CONTROL

WORKER INCREASES FREEDOM →

← AUTOCRATIC →   ← DEMOCRATIC →   ← "LET-ALONE" →

← LEADERSHIP STYLES →

How do we interpret that chart? At the extreme left side are leadership styles which focus almost all control with the leader. In this Autocratic style, the workers have little control, freedom, or voice: Theory X leadership. On the extreme right side is leadership given almost totally to the workers. The "official" top management has little voice, and leaves the workers alone to run things: Theory Y leadership.

Notice what occurs in the middle. Both the leader and the workers give up increasing amounts of control and freedom to the other, and a democratic style of leadership occurs. Leaders and workers respect each other and share authority. Teams abound. Leadership is shared in many areas, and centralized in others. All play a part. This middle area forms the core of the high-performance workplace.

Below is a situation and some directions, all drawn from Lackluster Video Company's past and present. Decide whether each of the directions is an example of Autocratic, Democratic, or "Let-Alone" leadership from the top. **Put an A, D, or L, depending on how you judge each statement.**

✍ THE LACKLUSTER SITUATION

As you remember, Lackluster has an immediate problem: the mix-up of Madonna videotapes put into cases marked for Disney children's sales. The problem clearly occurred in the assembly area. A short-term problem solving team has been created, and they are being given their "mission statement" by the President, Mrs. Vera Lackluster. Judge what leadership style she is using if she gives the following directions.

____ 1. "I sure hope you can solve this problem, because if you can't then Lackluster is sunk!"

____ 2. "You folks messed up bad somewhere! You'd better find out what your mistake was and fix it, or else . . . "

____ 3. "I'm sure you intelligent, energetic folks can solve this problem, now that it's your responsibility. I just *know* we won't have to find another assembly team."

____ 4. "We've got a problem and we're counting on you to take the lead in solving it. Let me know anything you need and we'll get it for you."

____ 5. "It's possible that you folks didn't make the mistake; it might have been that you got mistaken orders. If so, let me know; I'll make sure it never happens again."

____ 6. "Your task is to find out how to recover all the falsely-marked cases, in the next 4 days. I'll be on a cruise for the next two weeks, but write me a report on how you solved it."

Exercise 5F
LEADERSHIP IN A TEAM-BASED ENVIRONMENT

In this chapter you've been exploring three key aspects of people-to-people contact: one-on-one relationships, teams, and leadership. We have emphasized the roles of these three dynamics in a high-performance workplace. Now is your chance to put the theory into practice. We'll close this chapter with one final visit to the wacky world of Lackluster Video Company.

✍ LACKLUSTER: HIRING A NEW LEADER

The Lackluster team solved its short-term problem — all of the Madonna tapes are safely removed from Mickey Mouse cases. But now there's a different problem. Vera Lackluster, the company president, never came back from her cruise; she settled in Haiti. Consultant Deming has suggested that each work team review the top candidates for her job, and make a recommendation of which one they think would serve best in Lackluster's new high-performance workplace.

Here are the ratings of the top three candidates on 19 key traits, on a scale of 1 (low) to 5 (high). Decide which one you recommend, and explain your thinking. (Hint: First decide which leadership traits are most important in a high-performance environment.)

		RATINGS OF:		
RATED ON:		CURLY	MO	LARRY
1.	Spokesperson	4	3	4
2.	Catalyst	4	4	3
3.	Director	3	3	5
4.	Salesperson	5	3	4
5.	Coach	3	4	4
6.	Devil's advocate	3	3	5
7.	Servant	3	5	3
8.	Facilitator	4	5	3
9.	Cheerleader	3	4	3
10.	High energy	5	3	5
11.	Listens well	3	5	3
12.	Well organized	3	4	4
13.	Handles conflict	4	5	3
14.	Good judgment	3	4	4
15.	Persuasive	4	3	5
16.	Knowledgeable	5	3	5
17.	Respects others	3	5	3
18.	Encourages others	3	5	3
19.	Confident	3	3	5

WHICH ONE DO YOU RECOMMEND AS LACKLUSTER'S NEW LEADER? EXPLAIN WHY.

Exercise 5G
OTHER PEOPLE: MAKING YOUR MAP

This chapter, like the last ones, covered several mindful worker competencies. They were:

◊ Deal with others.

◊ Work in teams.

◊ Lead.

Once again, your job is to complete the profile of someone who is particularly competent with each of those competencies. Then you need to rate your own current competence, and set a goal for how competent you would like to be in that area 2-3 years from now.

✍ PROFILE OF SOMEONE EXCEPTIONALLY COMPETENT IN DEALING WITH OTHER PEOPLE:
Someone who can make other people feel at home and respected. Who can calm people down when they are upset. Someone who listens actively. Who can act (and be) comfortable with a wide variety of people in all sorts of situations.

Someone who:

Someone who:

✍ RATE YOUR OWN COMPETENCE AT DEALING WITH OTHER PEOPLE

HORRIBLE				FAIR					EXCELLENT
1	2	3	4	5	6	7	8	9	10

"X" point = current status   "Circle" point = 2-3 year goal

✍ WAYS TO *IMPROVE* YOUR COMPETENCE:

✍ WAYS TO *PROVE* YOUR COMPETENCE:

✍ PROFILE OF AN EXCEPTIONAL TEAM MEMBER: Someone who knows and can play the many different roles required on a team. Who can put team needs above personal needs. Someone who can balance people relations with task accomplishment.

Someone who:

Someone who:

✍ RATE YOUR OWN COMPETENCE AS A TEAM MEMBER

HORRIBLE				FAIR					EXCELLENT
1	2	3	4	5	6	7	8	9	10

"X" point = current status   "Circle" point = 2-3 year goal

✍ WAYS TO *IMPROVE* YOUR COMPETENCE:

✍ WAYS TO *PROVE* YOUR COMPETENCE:

✍ PROFILE OF AN EXCEPTIONAL LEADER: Someone who can inspire or convince others to work towards a given goal. Who can create a vision. Who can be effective when out in front of, supporting, or on a different path than those who follow.

Someone who:

Someone who:

✍ RATE YOUR OWN COMPETENCE AS A LEADER

HORRIBLE				FAIR					EXCELLENT
1	2	3	4	5	6	7	8	9	10

"X" point = current status   "Circle" point = 2-3 year goal

✍ **WAYS TO *IMPROVE* YOUR COMPETENCE:**

✍ **WAYS TO *PROVE* YOUR COMPETENCE:**

Summary Of Chapter 5
WHO ARE THOSE PEOPLE AND WHAT DO THEY WANT?

This chapter briefly explored interpersonal relationships, teams, and leadership. All three are important in the high performance workplace. Below, list some of the major ideas and insights you found in the Chapter.

✍ HERE ARE SOME KEY THINGS I LEARNED ABOUT PEOPLE IN THE WORKPLACE

◊

◊

◊

◊

◊

◊

◊

◊

◊

◊

Chapter 5 – Review Questions

1. Explore 'interpersonal relations': what it means, what we mean by *effective* interpersonal relations, and why it is important in the workplace. Use examples.

2. Explore how our work effectiveness is affected by others.

3. What are the disadvantages and advantages of working in teams in the workplace?

4. Examine possible team roles and what an individual might do to help a team function well.

5. What are the stages of team evolution? How do they work, and what might people feel during each stage?

6. Examine five of the behaviors associated with successful work teams.

7. How does the 'mindful worker' compare to the 'mindful work team'? Explain and use examples.

8. Explore what you mean by a leader, using examples.

9. What does the phrase, "Lead, follow, or get out of the way," imply about leadership? Use examples.

10. What are six characteristics that you believe are true of most leaders? Explain why.

11. Compare the similarities and differences between the roles of a leader in any of the following situations: leading individuals, teams, in a traditional workplace, in school settings, and/or social situations.

12. Compare Theory X versus Theory Y leadership: what they mean, how they work, what they believe about people, how they operate in the workplace, and how they fit in with high-performance workplaces.

13. How does interpersonal relationships, working with teams, and leading relate to each of the other competencies we have explored in this book?

CHAPTER 6

TELL ME AGAIN WHO YOU ARE

MINDFUL WORKER COMPETENCIES
EXPLORED IN CHAPTER 6

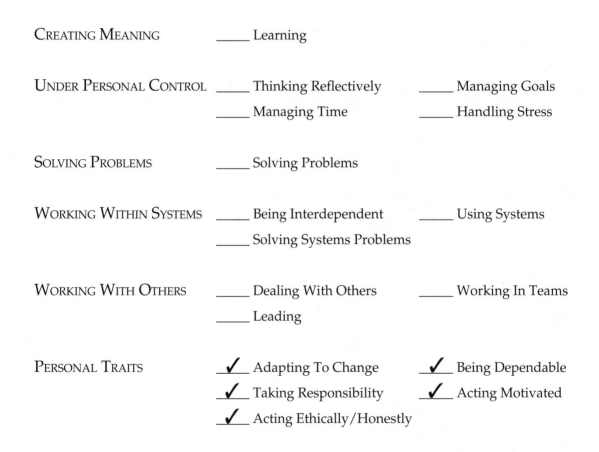

CREATING MEANING   _____ Learning

UNDER PERSONAL CONTROL   _____ Thinking Reflectively   _____ Managing Goals

     _____ Managing Time   _____ Handling Stress

SOLVING PROBLEMS   _____ Solving Problems

WORKING WITHIN SYSTEMS   _____ Being Interdependent   _____ Using Systems

     _____ Solving Systems Problems

WORKING WITH OTHERS   _____ Dealing With Others   _____ Working In Teams

     _____ Leading

PERSONAL TRAITS   ✔ Adapting To Change   ✔ Being Dependable

     ✔ Taking Responsibility   ✔ Acting Motivated

     ✔ Acting Ethically/Honestly

Introduction To Chapter 6
TELL ME AGAIN WHO YOU ARE . . .

Increasingly, high-performance workplaces will be hiring those who bring their heads to work: their knowledge, their skills, their abilities to work effectively in teams within systems, and the like.

There is another equally important aspect of the mindful worker, however: the character of the person. Some aspects will not be of major significance except in specific jobs: whether a person is outgoing or shy, calm or excitable, analytical or imaginative.

A few character traits, however, will clearly be in demand in all companies and jobs. Consider how important the following traits will be in the dynamic, demanding workplace of the 21st century:

"WE WANT PEOPLE WHO . . ."	TRAIT:
"Can adapt to change"	Flexibility
"Can be counted on"	Dependability
"Will shoulder the burden"	Responsibility
"Can be trusted"	Honesty
"Really want to perform"	Motivation

Do these sound like the kind of people you'd want on your sports team, . . . in your church, . . . to work beside, . . . to live beside? These are very much the kinds of traits employers want – and reward highly. They are key character traits of mindful workers.

A final warning. All of these character traits *can* be improved, but not quickly and not with just a few pages of a text. Like everything else, take this brief introduction and run with it.

Exercise 6A
"Can Adapt To Change" – Flexibility

"May you live in interesting times!" is an ancient Chinese wish. It is particularly interesting because, if we think about it a minute, we realize that it can be a blessing – or a curse. How can a wish be two things at once? What do you think?

✍ **"May You Live In Interesting Times"**

How can that be a blessing?

How can that be a curse?

There is a related saying which goes: "Change is good for those who are ready for it." Together, what do these quotes imply? In a world of much change, there is both danger and opportunity. You can end up somewhere that you don't want to be (e.g., a dead-end job, or unemployed), or you can figure out where you want to be and take advantage of the chaos to get there (many fortunes have been made in 'interesting times'). The difference in your destination? Partly luck and other factors, of course. But a lot of the difference is preparedness and your willingness to *take charge of change* rather than let it take charge of you.

Why is it hard for all of us to take charge of the changes that affect us? Some changes, of course, are immediately pleasant: putting a new piece of furniture in a house, riding in a new car, going out with a new friend, going to an interesting place for the first time.

Other changes are fairly neutral for us: we don't feel much one way or another. But many changes – and almost all of the big changes in our lives – bring some degree of fear and anxiety. Remember all the stressful factors we rated in Chapter 4? Why do they bring such stress, even if the end result becomes positive?

Think of some of the significant changes that you face, have faced, or will face: new jobs, new houses, new bosses, leaving home, getting married or divorced, having children, taking a first job, etc. Reflect on what made you nervous about those changes, and answer this question.

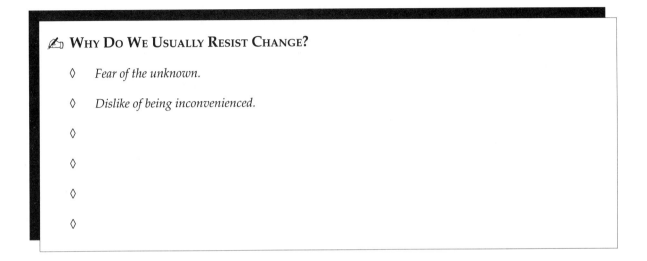

✐ Why Do We Usually Resist Change?

◊ *Fear of the unknown.*

◊ *Dislike of being inconvenienced.*

◊

◊

◊

◊

Such hesitations are natural, and they usually color almost all of our *initial* reactions to change. But then most of us adjust or hide our reactions and begin dealing with the changes. But we do this in different ways and degrees, and at different rates. Look at the following typical ways to react to change, and see if you can spot your typical reactions and those of others you know.

Some Styles Of Reacting To Change

◊ Go Along – be pulled along by the change, muttering and griping.

◊ Adapt – change your ways so that you fit in with the change.

◊ Resist – fight to make the change go away, or adapt to *you*.

◊ Avoid – get out of the way of the change, if you can.

◊ Manipulate – lead the change and make it do what you want it to do.

◊ Deny – ignore the change and pretend that it's not there.

Following are some situations about people dealing with change. See if you can label each of their behaviors in terms of one of the reaction styles on the previous page. You *might* find cases where more than one style is used. Write the style(s) in the blanks before each person's reactions.

The Grants have three children: Arnie, Amy, and Bernie. After years of strife, the Grants have broken the news to their children that they will be seeking a divorce. Here's how the children and Mr. Grant react.

---

1. Amy goes all quiet. She says very little, and will never even respond to discussion of the divorce.

2. Mr. Grant speaks calmly of the divorce, but is very often especially affectionate to his wife. He often surprises everyone by discussing plans for the whole family: a family vacation, a new room on the house, a visit to their grandparents, etc.

3. Bernie has spent 3 weeks crying sometimes, trying to argue his parents out of it sometimes, and asking deep questions about what's going to happen sometimes.

4. Arnie throws screaming tantrums for 3 solid weeks, in school and at home. It's impossible to calm him down.

The Baldspot Hair Treatment Company announces that it is going to move its offices to Toupee, a small town 45 miles from the current offices. This move will combine several smaller offices and will create a new organizational structure with some different types of jobs. Several of Baldspot's current employees react to the move.

---

5. Ernie Young immediately protests loudly; he *likes* it where he is. He eventually goes along with the move, but frequently comments on how unfair it was.

6. Shelly Butterworth rents an apartment in Toupee, joins the Chamber of Commerce, and expresses interest in a more challenging job assignment.

7. Ed Smoot starts job-hunting, and eventually finds a similar job (for less pay), without having to move.

8. Emerson McBee joins the early griping, but then makes the move. He keeps doing his same old job, but does not seem to be as interested or productive in it.

9. Laverne White commutes to Toupee for the next several years, initially only until she found another job, but then 'just because I got used to the commute.'

Many different people and many reactions to the same changes. It's not always easy to predict *how* we will react to specific changes in our lives, but all of us do have general patterns. See if you can assess your own patterns – and those of some of your friends and relatives. Write three names (or initials) at the top of the three blank columns below. Then rate your own change-reaction styles and those of the three people you're thinking of.

✍ HOW DO YOU RATE?

Here are some ways to react to change:	Yourself	_____	_____	_____
1. GO ALONG.	____	____	____	____
2. ADAPT.	____	____	____	____
3. RESIST.	____	____	____	____
4. AVOID.	____	____	____	____
5. MANIPULATE.	____	____	____	____
6. DENY.	____	____	____	____

(Rating Scale: O = Often   S = Sometimes   N = Not like that)

It's not too easy to rate yourself accurately, is it? Most of us want to believe that we are reasonably competent at dealing with change. And, in fact, most of us *can* adjust reasonably well to change – eventually. But that last word is the key. Highly flexible people can generally adjust to change rapidly, while those who are less flexible can take a lot longer to adjust.

One factor which makes it both easy and hard to adjust to change is the *unknown*. We fear the unknown, and so we tend to fear change because we don't know what the results will be, or the consequences for us. Yet this also makes it easier to accept change! Why? Because frequently we go along with something that seems minor, and only later realize how much impact it is going to have on us. A prime example is the xerox machine: seemingly a very positive change, yet this one invention has probably changed the nature and organization of business, government, and education as anything else in this century. Here's a chance for you to stretch your insights into the unknown:

AN INSIGHT INTO THE UNKNOWN

FAIRLY SOON, COMPUTERS AND SCREENS WILL PROBABLY BE BUILT INTO ALMOST EVERY TELEPHONE. HOW WILL THIS AFFECT YOU, POSITIVELY AND NEGATIVELY?

We discussed the notion that one of the differences between flexible and inflexible people is the *speed* with which they adjust to change. A business researcher named Kenneth Blanchard has expanded on that notion. Below is a chart he has developed to show a very important factor: *certain types of adjustments almost always take longer than others*. Take a look at his chart.

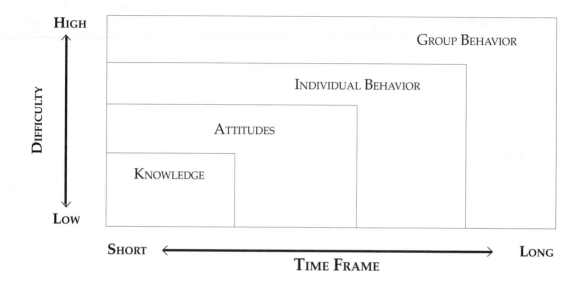

What does this chart say to us about change? Basically that our knowledge is the quickest factor to change, and our group behavior is the slowest factor to change. Also that the speed with which any of these factors change is very much influenced by the difficulty involved.

Let's take young Bernie Grant and the divorce as an example. Fairly early he may learn to intellectually understand the nature and implications of the divorce. It will take longer for his feelings to adjust. Even then he won't be able to adjust his behavior until later. And only after a long time (assuming everyone else makes it through those stages) will he be able to behave in an adjusted/accepting way about the di-

vorce with his family. Change takes time. Different types of change take different amounts of time.

One final question about this idea of flexibility and change. Let's suppose that the Baldspot Hair Treatment Company not only changed towns; they changed management styles. Their traditional management converted to the need for a high-performance management style: systems thinking, team emphasis, lifelong learning, etc. Think about the implications and answer this question.

HOW DOES BLANCHARD'S VIEW OF CHANGE DYNAMICS RELATE TO CREATING AND WORKING IN HIGH-PERFORMANCE FIRMS?

Exercise 6B
"CAN BE COUNTED ON" – DEPENDABILITY

Ever waited on the sidewalk for someone to pick you up, and they never came? Ever had someone promise absolutely to pay you back the money they owed you "by tomorrow morning," but they never did? Ever made part of some arrangements, then found out that someone else never made their part, so the whole thing fell through? Then you've dealt with the issue of dependability.

Let's start by getting our terms clear. See if you can figure out the differences between these three similar (but different) words below:

Someone is **dependable** if they:

Someone takes **responsibility** if they:

Someone is **honest** if they:

No one is *totally* dependable. The conflicts and pressures of our lives make it certain that from time to time we fail to follow through *completely* on things we have promised or implied that we will do. Why is that? Let's see if we can come up with some of the variables that affect our dependability in particular situations. Below are two factors which might have an impact; see if you can identify some other factors that sometimes influence dependability.

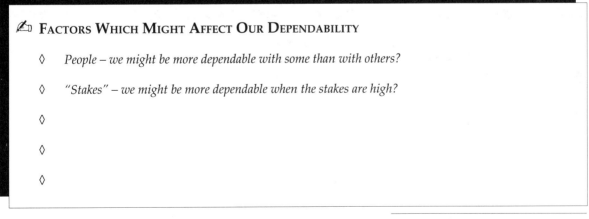

FACTORS WHICH MIGHT AFFECT OUR DEPENDABILITY

◊ *People – we might be more dependable with some than with others?*

◊ *"Stakes" – we might be more dependable when the stakes are high?*

◊

◊

◊

Our exact degree of dependability might depend on the specific person we are dealing with: our closest friend, or someone we really dislike, for example. But as you've noted above it might also depend on the situation. We might be a little more dependable with a close friend on the job (where the stakes were seen as very high) than in a social situation (where the stakes might not be nearly as high). Let's put some of those factors together. Below, prioritize how dependable you think most people are in these situations: 1 means most dependable and 5 means least dependable.

✍ **HOW DEPENDABLE DO YOU THINK PEOPLE *USUALLY* ARE IN THESE SITUATIONS?**
(Rank them 1-5, with 1 being most dependable)

_____ How dependable are people with their friends?

_____ How dependable are people on the job?

_____ How dependable are people at school?

_____ How dependable are people with their family?

_____ How dependable are people with strangers?

The work you've done above on dependability makes one important assumption: that dependability involves other people. Certainly that is true *most* of the time. *'Dependability' often implies that others are depending on us.* When we are undependable, we are letting them down. But do you think that's *always* the case?

We make or imply promises to others, but we also make them to ourselves. We sometimes don't carry out our promise to others in the fullest possible way: we're not fully dependable. But how about when we don't carry out our internal promise to the fullest? Try your hand at the following question.

✍ **HAVE YOU BEEN UNDEPENDABLE IF YOU HAVE BROKEN A PROMISE TO YOURSELF? EXPLAIN YOUR ANSWER.**

Mostly, people won't be aware whether or not you have kept a promise you made to yourself. But they will be quite aware of how dependable you are in terms of your obligations to other people. You will gradually get a reputation for being dependable or undependable, and this reputation may follow you around like a shadow.

How do people decide if you're dependable or not?

Partly it is a matter of keeping or breaking specific promises: picking someone up, doing a chore, completing a project, passing along a message, etc. Often, though, dependability is a matter of going by the unwritten or understood 'rules of the game.' We (and others) just know what's expected of us. Following is an opportunity to explore some of those unwritten rules for the working world. A couple of examples are given. See how many more you can come up with.

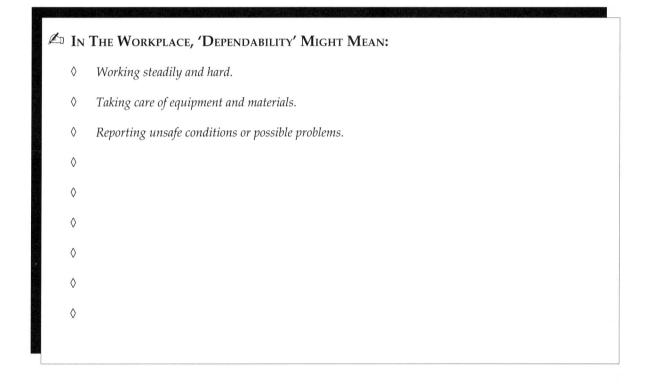

✍ IN THE WORKPLACE, 'DEPENDABILITY' MIGHT MEAN:

◊ *Working steadily and hard.*

◊ *Taking care of equipment and materials.*

◊ *Reporting unsafe conditions or possible problems.*

◊

◊

◊

◊

◊

◊

There are many unwritten rules in the working world, aren't there? Break many of them, very often, and the reputation for 'undependable' might start creeping towards you. But there's one other thing to notice about these unwritten rules. Do they only apply to the workplace or are they more generalized? Try this question:

How many of the above 'unwritten' rules *also* apply to school?

You probably noticed that almost all of the same rules apply to both the workplace and the classroom. This might give you a fairly good way to measure how you are going to perform in the workplace – by making a frank assessment of how you perform in the classroom.

Why do employers put so much emphasis on de-pendability? Obviously there's a lot at stake for the employer. The employer might lose money, face a lawsuit, or some such because of employees' undependability. But think of *who else* might pay the price of a worker's lack of dependability. Below are some situations where one worker acts in an unde-pendable way. For each one, think of an example of how a co-worker might have to 'pay the price.'

✍ **WHO 'PAYS THE PRICE' FOR A WORKER'S UNDEPENDABLE ACTION . . .**

1.   . . . when a worker is absent on inventory day?

     Three team members must stay late to do the extra work.

2.   . . . when a worker does not report an unsafe machine?

3.   . . . when a worker does not follow instructions on a new procedure?

4.   . . . when a worker lets scrap parts accumulate around her work area?

5.   . . . when a worker comes to work hung-over?

6.   . . . when a worker spreads rumors about other workers and supervisors?

Clearly we pay the price for other's undependability — and they pay the price for our undependability. The price may be minor (such as being late because someone forgot to pick us up). Often the price is major (injury, major loss, or worse). As a closer to this topic of dependability, try this question.

Is 'dependability' more important in a tradi-tional or a high performance workplace? Why?

Exercise 6C
"WILL SHOULDER THE BURDEN" – TAKING RESPONSIBILITY

A recent study asked a number of people to describe the meaning of the term 'responsibility.' All of their descriptions contained some or all of these factors:

◊ COMMITMENT – an agreement between yourself and others.

◊ AUTHORITY – some sense of moral or actual authority to carry something out.

◊ ACTION – something will occur which you are responsible for.

◊ ACCOUNTABILITY – assignment of praise or blame to you.

◊ LEADERSHIP – influencing events and people to achieve something.

"Taking responsibility" seems to include pieces of all five of these things. But it seems that the exact mixture of these ingredients shifts from situation to situation. Examine the following situations and decide which aspects of responsibility are emphasized. The first one is completed as an example.

◊ **"Okay, you're responsible for bringing the drinks for the party."**

This situation seems to emphasize: commitment ('we've got a deal'), action ('go buy the drinks and transport them'), and accountability ('we know who to be mad at if it doesn't happen'). Significant authority and leadership don't seem to be necessary in this case.

◊ **"I'll be out of town all next week and you'll be responsible for things."**

✍

◊ **"I'm holding you responsible for the behavior of your friends tonight!"**

✍

◊ **"She's super! She just automatically assumes responsibility around here."**

✍

Are there any of the five elements that you felt were common to all of these situations? If there were, they probably included the ideas of commitment and accountability. Those seem to be very close to the core of responsibility.

Why do people assume responsibility for things? Often the labor and risks are much higher than any explicit rewards, yet people continue to accept responsibility. If you're ordered to do something at work, or if it's part of your job, that's one thing. But how about in personal situations? Here are some of the common reasons people give for volunteering to take responsibility.

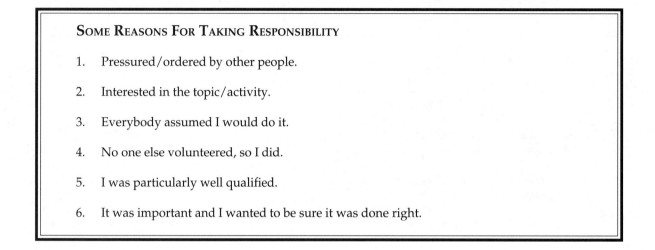

SOME REASONS FOR TAKING RESPONSIBILITY

1. Pressured/ordered by other people.

2. Interested in the topic/activity.

3. Everybody assumed I would do it.

4. No one else volunteered, so I did.

5. I was particularly well qualified.

6. It was important and I wanted to be sure it was done right.

Do these kinds of reasons fit with your experience of being responsible for things? Let's make sure. Following, list at least five times when you have been responsible for something significant.

✎ _____ 1.

✎ _____ 2.

✎ _____ 3.

✎ _____ 4.

✎ _____ 5.

In front of each of those items write the numbers (from the list above) of *why* you were responsible for those things. If they don't fit, put the number "7" and figure out what led you to take responsibility for that thing.

Your responses to the previous activity should give you some idea of your pattern of volunteering to take responsibility for things. If most or all of your reasons were "1," then you might want to work on volunteering to take responsibility for things. That might help strengthen your abilities and experiences in that important area of mindful working.

The *costs and risks* of taking responsibility are mostly obvious. The costs include time, energy, and worry. The risks mostly relate to the results of failing to carrying out your responsibility adequately: letting others down, embarrassment, guilt, blame, etc. But what about the *benefits* of taking responsibility? Speak for yourself, by answering this question.

✍ **WHAT ARE THE POSSIBLE BENEFITS OF TAKING RESPONSIBILITY?**

This idea of taking responsibility is not a minor topic. When we look closely, we realize that the ways most of our social institutions operate are based on assumptions about responsibility. Following are some important types of social institutions. What do they assume about who takes responsibility for what? See how many assumptions you can find; a few are given.

WHAT ASSUMPTIONS ABOUT RESPONSIBILITY ARE MADE BY OUR:

CRIMINAL JUSTICE SYSTEM?

◊ *That most citizens will 'police their own behavior.'*

◊ *That citizens should not take responsibility for being 'judge, jury, and executioner' - e.g., a lynch mob.*

◊ ✍

◊ ✍

◊ ✍

◊ ✍

Health System?

◊ 🖎

◊ *That responsibility for diagnosing and treating important illnesses must be given only to those with certain licenses.*

◊ 🖎

◊ *That 'the medical community' has a responsibility to discover and make available increasingly sophisticated (and expensive) ways to treat patients.*

◊ 🖎

◊ 🖎

◊ 🖎

◊ 🖎

Business System?

◊ *That supervisors must be responsible for employee's work activities.*

◊ *That middle- and top-management can effectively be responsible for determining the best production methods and procedures.*

◊ 🖎

◊ 🖎

School System?

◊ 🖎

◊ *That responsibility for assuring that learning takes place must rest with the teacher.*

◊ *That students cannot assume their own responsibility for deciding what subjects to study throughout their education.*

◊ 🖎

◊ 🖎

The idea of "taking responsibility" does indeed influence many of our institutions and systems, doesn't it? In fact, it can be argued that most of the rules and understandings that govern our lives are based on notions of who can, will, and should take responsibility for various things.

Let's get one final look at this idea of taking responsibility, and give you some insights into why it is such an important concept for you. Let's consider how things would be if we had very different assumptions about responsibility. See what you can do with these two possibilities.

✍ WHAT WOULD IT BE LIKE IF?

Business assumed that all workers would take full responsibility for their own performance?

Schools assumed that all students would take full responsibility for their own performance?

Both businesses and schools would be very different places if they operated in a way which gave workers and learners full opportunity to assume their own responsibility. Would they be *better* places? More enjoyable, challenging, and fulfilling places? Probably so, in many ways. Are they going to become more that type of place in the future? The workplace almost certainly will, as businesses adopt high-performance viewpoints and develop mindful workers. The school system? The crystal ball is less clear on that question . . .

Exercise 6D
"CAN BE TRUSTED" – HONESTY

Mark Twain said, "Always do right. That will gratify some people and astonish the rest!" The cynical and optimistic views of human nature have collided throughout human history. The issue of honesty is a particularly important point of disagreement between traditional and high-performance managers. Theory X and Theory Y management essentially disagree on this issue. Authority and control are handed over, or withheld, based on this issue.

A dictionary definition of honesty goes something like this: "honorable in your beliefs and actions." But that may be too general for our purposes. Let's approach this idea of honesty from another direction. Below are some familiar statements. Rate each of them.

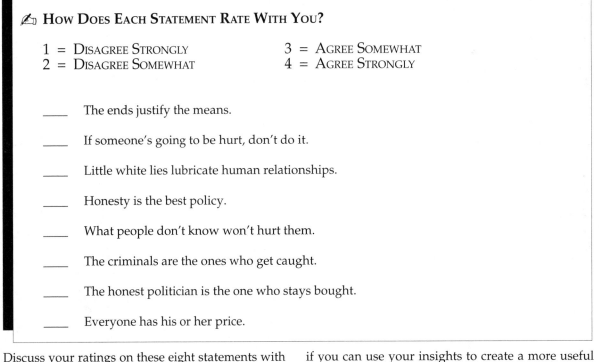

✍ HOW DOES EACH STATEMENT RATE WITH YOU?

1 = DISAGREE STRONGLY   3 = AGREE SOMEWHAT
2 = DISAGREE SOMEWHAT   4 = AGREE STRONGLY

_____ The ends justify the means.

_____ If someone's going to be hurt, don't do it.

_____ Little white lies lubricate human relationships.

_____ Honesty is the best policy.

_____ What people don't know won't hurt them.

_____ The criminals are the ones who get caught.

_____ The honest politician is the one who stays bought.

_____ Everyone has his or her price.

Discuss your ratings on these eight statements with others. Share your viewpoints and reasons. Then see if you can use your insights to create a more useful definition of honesty.

✍ "HONESTY" MEANS:

Some people believe that honesty is an absolute value, to be followed under all circumstances. Others argue that it can be somewhat relative in actual practice, depending on the situation. It is important that you have a firm sense of where you actually stand on the issue of honesty. The following activity is designed to help you do that.

A number of situations are listed below. Rate each one, using the scale provided. It may sound silly to say in an exercise on honesty, but **be honest in your ratings**. You won't have to share these with others, so put down what you actually think about each situation.

✍ HOW ACCEPTABLE IS IT TO:

1 = OKAY   2 = OFTEN OKAY   3 = USUALLY NOT OKAY   4 = NEVER

_____ 1.   Do things a little less well to get finished by lunch time.

_____ 2.   Don't confront or report a co-worker who is stealing.

_____ 3.   Take personal days off and call them sick leave.

_____ 4.   Go along with overcharging a customer when it's safe.

_____ 5.   Leave work early when the supervisor is not there.

_____ 6.   Quit right at quitting time even if you're not finished with something and the project won't get done on time.

_____ 7.   Take small amounts of paper and pens home with you from work.

_____ 8.   Make copies of computer software for your own personal use.

_____ 9.   Do private work on the side that could be done by the company.

_____ 10. Toss good stuff away with trash so you don't have to sort it.

_____ 11. Use the company vehicle for personal business occasionally.

_____ 12. Work on personal projects during work time.

_____ 13. Don't confront a co-worker who's falsifying quality figures.

_____ 14. Take leave at hunting season even if it's rush time at work.

_____ 15. Sell defective materials in order to make your quota.

So what's the pattern of your sense of honesty, based on your answers above? For guidance, add up all of your numbers. The higher the number, the stronger your sense of honesty might be. Someone who feels that honesty is an absolute would score a 60. Someone who felt that "anything goes" would score a 15. Where do you fit?

The issue of workforce honesty has been an important one for businesses ever since the first businesses began. Many retail merchants in ancient times, for example, hired two separate guards: one to watch for customer theft, and one to watch for employee theft!

As American business and industry are changing their ways in order to remain competitive, the question of honesty may also be taking on different dimensions. Let's examine that possibility.

Cashmart is a major discount store, begun by an Alabama business genius named Slim Cashton. It is now a nationwide chain of stores, handling all sorts of merchandise at economical prices. It has dozens of employees in each store, many of whom are part-time. It has millions of dollars worth of goods coming in the back doors and going out the front doors each month. The managers are considering moving to a high-performance style of management, with all that implies. Much authority and responsibility given to employee teams, more reliance on inspection of processes, systems thinking, and a spirit of interdependence. Less reliance on traditional forms of supervision and protection. These managers have asked you, as a management consultant, to examine how the two forms of management will differ in terms of issues relating to employee honesty.

Your consultant team thinks this situation through, then fills in an analysis of consequences like the one below. Some examples are given to help you get started.

✍ HONESTY/DISHONESTY WITH A TRADITIONAL MANAGEMENT STYLE

What might be lost from employee dishonesty?
◊   *Unreported damage to equipment.*

What is the probability of that occurring?

How does the company guard against such dishonesty?

What are the 'hidden costs' of such safeguards?
◊   *Employees, not being trusted, don't give as much to the company.*

✍ Honesty/Dishonesty With A High-Performance Management Style

What might be lost from employee dishonesty?
◊   *Unreported damage to equipment.*

What is the probability of that occurring?

How does the company safeguard against such dishonesty?

What are the 'hidden costs' of such safeguards?

Did you observe the changes that occurred as you shifted from a traditional to a high-performance management style? With more employee authority, employee teams, less supervision, less quality inspection, and the like, the company left itself much more open to the consequences of employee dishonesty. At least they left themselves without many of the traditional safeguards: fewer supervisors, less supervisory control, less inspections, and so forth.

But in return they received one – and possibly two – major benefits. The first one was fewer direct costs of safeguards. Fewer supervisor hours and less paperwork and other methods designed mainly to frustrate employee dishonesty. The other possible benefit? It *could* be far greater than the first benefit, because it *could* cut down dramatically on the frequency, and thus the costs, of employee dishonesty. That possibility? Explore it – and its possible payoffs – by answering the following questions.

✍ If The Workforce Has More Control Over Their Work . . .

Might they be more honest?

Might they assure others' honesty?

How likely is this to happen?

Clearly, those companies moving towards high-performance management styles are gambling that employees who feel a greater and more personal stake in their work and their company will voluntarily act in an honest manner. Moreover, they expect that they will take more responsibility for assuring that their co-workers are also more honest on the job.

There is considerable evidence that this is, in fact, occurring. And it makes sense. Human beings tend to be more protective of what is their own than they usually do of what belongs to others.

Imagine yourself working for Cashmans. If you felt that you were 'just a hired hand,' how concerned would you be about employee dishonesty (your own and others')? Would that change if you felt that you were 'part of the team,' with a real stake in the store's success? Let's find out, by putting you in Cashman's and revisiting some questions you answered earlier.

You're now a member of a work team at Cashman's. Your team members are the people around you: your classmates. Think about working in a situation where you make decisions as a group, supervise yourselves, set goals for yourselves, and share in store profits. Cashmans' is no longer 'their store.' It is 'our store.' In that context, rate the following statements.

✐ How Acceptable Is It For You To:

1 = Okay   2 = Often Okay   3 = Usually Not Okay   4 = Not Okay

____ 1. Do things a little less well to get finished by lunch time.
____ 2. Don't confront a team member who is stealing.
____ 3. Take personal days off and call them sick leave.
____ 4. Go along with overcharging a customer when it's safe.
____ 5. Leave work early when today's team leader is not there.
____ 6. Quit right at quitting time even if you're not finished with something and the project won't get done on time.
____ 7. Take small amounts of paper and pens home with you from work.
____ 8. Make copies of computer software for your own personal use.
____ 9. Do private work on the side that could be done by the company.
____ 10. Toss good stuff away with trash so you don't have to sort it.
____ 11. Use the company vehicle for personal business occasionally.
____ 12. Work on personal projects during work time.
____ 13. Don't confront a team member who's falsifying quality figures.
____ 14. Take leave at hunting season even if it's rush time at work.
____ 15. Sell defective materials in order to make your quota.

After you've finished rating these items, once again add up all of your numbers. Then compare it to the total you had two pages ago. If it's higher, then this indicates that you would be *more* inclined to act with strict honesty (and to insist on similar behavior from others) in a team environment than in a traditional work environment. Doesn't it make sense? We're more careful with those we know, those we depend on, and those who depend on us. That's what the high-performance companies are hoping for in mindful workers.

Exercise 6E
"REALLY WANTS TO PERFORM" – MOTIVATION

Carrots, sticks, dreams, power, gold, love, hate, fear, eagerness – the list of motivators seems endless. Employers, coaches, and teachers all point to motivation as one of the highest values – the difference between success and failure, winning and losing, contributing or undercutting. Yet they also acknowledge that it is one of the most difficult of attributes to develop – in a student, a ball player, or a worker.

What *is* this magical characteristic? A simple definition of motivation might be: "the encouragement to act with a purpose." Yet that definition really avoids the key question. What is it that encourages people to act with a purpose? Why will one student study and the next will not? Why will the person who does not study still work hard on the job? Why will neither of them vote? Why will both of them get involved in community improvement projects? Motivation is a puzzle, and at best we can only scratch the edges of it.

WHERE DOES MOTIVATION COME FROM?

Obviously, motivation can be positive or negative: the carrot or the stick. Either can be used to get the donkey to go where you want it to go. Yet a more interesting view of the source of motivation comes from the idea of internal versus external sources of motivation. Here are the two sources. Read each one, and then think of several examples from the classroom and the workplace. Some examples are given.

EXTERNAL MOTIVATION

External means outside, and external motivation refers to the encouragements that we receive from outside of ourselves. To look at external motivators, look for those forces (positive or negative) made available to us by people or events beyond ourselves. Fill in some examples below.

✐ EXAMPLES OF EXTERNAL MOTIVATORS

IN SCHOOL:

◊ *Grades*

IN THE WORKPLACE:

◊ *Salary*

INTERNAL MOTIVATION

Internal motivators refer to those sources of encouragement to act which arise from within our inner selves. They may be influenced by external factors, but basically they are those messages we send to our own minds and hearts. To discover internal motivators, look to the ways in which you are talking to yourself about what to do. Fill in some examples below.

✍ **EXAMPLES OF INTERNAL MOTIVATORS**

IN SCHOOL:
◊ *Desire to learn something.*

IN THE WORKPLACE:
◊ *Pride in your work.*

Do you sense the difference between these two types of motivators? Either one can be positive or negative. Either one can be effective sometimes. But stop and think about what motivates *you*. Are you more motivated by internal or external motivators?

For most people the internal motivators tend to be more reliable and effective on a day-to-day basis. As a matter of fact, internal motivators can often be so strong that they resist *massive* counter pressures from external motivators. Here are a couple of examples; see if you can add three other examples.

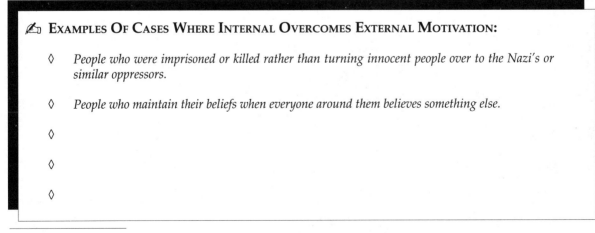

✍ **EXAMPLES OF CASES WHERE INTERNAL OVERCOMES EXTERNAL MOTIVATION:**

◊ *People who were imprisoned or killed rather than turning innocent people over to the Nazi's or similar oppressors.*

◊ *People who maintain their beliefs when everyone around them believes something else.*

◊

◊

◊

Throughout this book we've explored two types of companies and management styles: traditional, and high-performance. It should come as no surprise that traditional management styles tend to emphasize use of **external** motivators, while high performance management styles tend to emphasize use of **internal** motivators. It's not very hard to tell the difference in styles, as this example will show.

Following is a short passage from an actual advertisement mailed out to business educators and managers. Your task is to read the passage, then do two things. First, decide which management style this person reflects. Second, rewrite the passage to make it appeal to the motivation concerns of the *other* management style.

"WHAT TO SAY TO SHAPE UP THE PEOPLE WHO WORK FOR YOU"

"I'm going to show you how you can immediately straighten out problem employees — and fight back against their absenteeism, gold bricking, insubordination, complaints, and bad habits.

My name is W. H. Weiss. I've been in management for over 42 years and I'm going to show you 160 powerful secrets you can use to motivate the people who work for you — and rebut the excuses, alibis, and threats you're likely to hear . . ."

That ad shows a Theory ____ management approach to motivation.

Now it's your turn to write an advertisement. In the box below, write an alternative passage that would appeal to those trying the other management approach to workforce motivation. Be Creative!

✍ "WHAT TO SAY TO HELP YOUR WORKFORCE DO THEIR BEST"

MOTIVATION: WHAT DO WE NEED?

Mr. W. H. Weiss obviously believes in the power of the threat, backed up by a Theory X philosophy of management. In fact, his approach fits with some important research concerning human needs. Abraham Maslow spent years conducting research on human needs and has established a very important theory called "Maslow's Hierarchy of Needs." Dr. Maslow believes that we have five different levels of needs, which look like this:

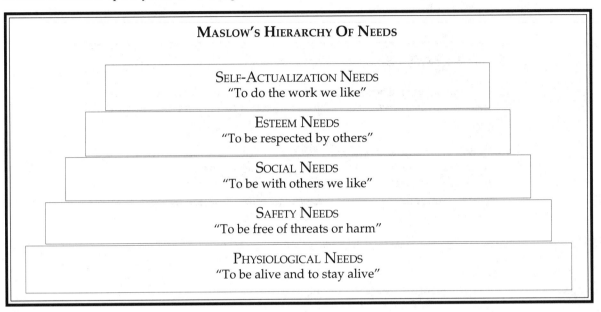

What does this hierarchy mean? It means that we have five levels of needs, and that the bottom level is the most important, the next level the second most important, and so forth. Maslow believed that human beings must first satisfy their most basic needs for food, shelter, etc. Only then can we worry about our second level of need. And so forth. Notice the qualitative differences in these levels of need. Make some comparisons; a couple of examples are given.

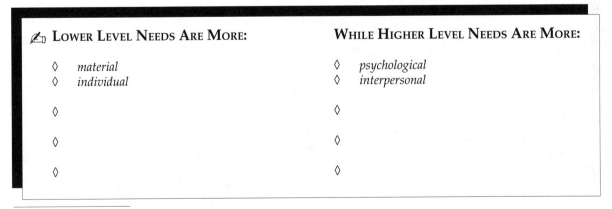

 LOWER LEVEL NEEDS ARE MORE:	WHILE HIGHER LEVEL NEEDS ARE MORE:
◊ *material*	◊ *psychological*
◊ *individual*	◊ *interpersonal*
◊	◊
◊	◊
◊	◊

Let's explore this idea of levels of needs and motivation a little bit. Below are listed some of the factors which *might* motivate students to work hard and do well in school. Add several more possible factors based on your experience.

✍ **POSSIBLE MOTIVATORS FOR SCHOOL EFFORT AND SUCCESS**

1. Wanting to get good grades.

2. Wanting to do the very best you can.

3. Fear of what others might say if you do poorly.

4. Desire to qualify for the best possible job.

5.

6.

7.

8.

Now think about what kinds of motivators each of those factors actually is. What human need does "wanting to get good grades" meet? Perhaps social needs (if the underlying concern is others' approval), or perhaps self-actualization (if good grades are truly a symbol of your own pride in achievement). Could it be an effort to meet safety needs? Possibly.

Match the school motivators above to Maslow's Hierarchy.

Now let's move this exploration into the workplace, by going back to our Theory X manager, W. H. Weiss. He advocates threats, mistrust, suspicion, and the like.

WHICH LEVELS OF MASLOW'S HIERARCHY DOES W. H. WEISS APPEAL TO?

Manager Weiss, having cut his teeth on traditional workplaces, naturally sees employees as 'hands.' 'Hands' need food, shelter, safety, and things like that, don't they? Look at your own hands. Do you really care whether or not they like people, or want to be respected, or need to feel good about the things you tell them to do? Of course not. You don't motivate hands by appealing to their minds or hearts or souls.

But what if you're hiring 'heads' instead of 'hands'? What if you're a high-performance workplace? Then you care very much about the mindful worker's feelings and thoughts and more sophisticated needs.

Mindful workers – the special types of people so valuable in the high performance workplace – can find plenty of jobs which will satisfy their more basic needs. That's true even in the tightest economy. So the motivating factors to be concerned with are the higher levels, involving things like respect, teamwork, meaningful tasks, responsibility, and the like.

Below are a list of factors which researchers believe affect workers' motivation. Of the sixteen factors, check **eight** of them which you feel most often will lead workers to feel satisfied with their jobs.

✍ WHICH EIGHT FACTORS CONTRIBUTE MOST TO JOB MOTIVATION?

_____ 1. Personal growth

_____ 2. Working conditions

_____ 3. Job security

_____ 4. Sense of achievement

_____ 5. Company policies

_____ 6. Relationship with peers

_____ 7. Recognition

_____ 8. Relationship with supervisors

_____ 9. Advancement opportunities

_____ 10. The work itself

_____ 11. Supervision

_____ 12. Responsibility

_____ 13. Job status

_____ 14. Personal life

_____ 15. Salary

_____ 16. Relationship with subordinates

These sixteen factors are found in a research study published by Harvard University. The researchers found, in fact, that only six of the factors were high motivators (numbers 1, 4, 7, 9, 10, and 12). Two of them (15 and 16) were 'break-even' items. The remaining eight were in fact factors which tended to lead towards job dissatisfaction and lack of motivation.

Match the high-motivating factors with Maslow's Hierarchy.

See what this research is saying? It suggests that American workers seem to be getting their lower-level needs met. They are increasingly seeking work and working conditions that meet their higher level needs.

Which brings us to the final question in this chapter on success oriented behavior patterns.

WHAT MOTIVATES YOU TO WORK?

Exercise 6F
KEY PERSONAL TRAITS: MAKING YOUR MAP

In this chapter we have dealt with the following five competencies of the mindful worker:

◊ Adapt to change.

◊ Be dependable.

◊ Take responsibility.

◊ Act ethically.

◊ Act motivated.

Once again, add to the profile of an exceptional person, then use that to rate your current competency, set your goals, and plan ahead.

✍ PROFILE OF SOMEONE EXCEPTIONALLY ABLE TO ADAPT TO CHANGE: Someone who takes the unusual in stride. Who does not 'hang on' to old things just because they're comfortable. Who sees opportunities where others see threats. Someone who enjoys adjusting systems, activities, and patterns to fit new situations.

Someone who:

Someone who:

✍ RATE YOUR OWN COMPETENCE AT ADJUSTING TO CHANGE

HORRIBLE				FAIR					EXCELLENT
1	2	3	4	5	6	7	8	9	10

"X" point = current status   "Circle" point = 2-3 year goal

✍ WAYS TO *IMPROVE* YOUR COMPETENCE:

✍ WAYS TO *PROVE* YOUR COMPETENCE:

✍ PROFILE OF SOMEONE WHO IS EXCEPTIONALLY DEPENDABLE: Someone who always accomplishes what was promised or expected. Who can be given a task without hesitation or checking up. Who doesn't let others or themselves down by not coming through.

Someone who:

Someone who:

✍ RATE YOUR OWN COMPETENCE AT DEPENDABILITY

HORRIBLE   FAIR   EXCELLENT

    1   2   3   4   5   6   7   8   9   10

    "X" point = current status   "Circle" point = 2-3 year goal

---

✍ WAYS TO *IMPROVE* YOUR COMPETENCE:

✍ WAYS TO *PROVE* YOUR COMPETENCE:

✍ PROFILE OF SOMEONE WHO IS EXCEPTIONALLY ABLE TO ASSUME RESPONSIBILITY: Someone who can be counted on to see what needs to be done – and to do it whether asked or not. Who cannot or will not walk away from burdens or tasks.

Someone who:

Someone who:

✍ RATE YOUR OWN COMPETENCE AT TAKING RESPONSIBILITY

HORRIBLE				FAIR				EXCELLENT
1	2	3	4	5	6	7	8	9	10

"X" point = current status   "Circle" point = 2-3 year goal

✍ WAYS TO *IMPROVE* YOUR COMPETENCE:

✍ WAYS TO *PROVE* YOUR COMPETENCE:

✍ PROFILE OF SOMEONE WHO ACTS WITH EXCEPTIONAL HONESTY: Someone who has high moral standards and lives up to them. Who can be counted on to be truthful. Someone who guards the property, rights, and reputation of others.

Someone who:

Someone who:

✍ RATE YOUR OWN COMPETENCE IN ACTING HONESTLY

HORRIBLE   FAIR   EXCELLENT

| 1 | 2 | 3 | 4 | 5 | 6 | 7 | 8 | 9 | 10 |

"X" point = current status   "Circle" point = 2-3 year goal

✍ WAYS TO *IMPROVE* YOUR COMPETENCE:

✍ WAYS TO *PROVE* YOUR COMPETENCE:

✍ PROFILE OF SOMEONE WHO IS EXCEPTIONALLY MOTIVATED: Someone who is enthusiastic about things. Who throws themselves into ventures and makes them successful. Someone who sees the need to commit, to work hard, and to make things happen.

Someone who:

Someone who:

✍ RATE YOUR OWN COMPETENCE AT ACTING MOTIVATED

HORRIBLE				FAIR					EXCELLENT
1	2	3	4	5	6	7	8	9	10

"X" point = current status   "Circle" point = 2-3 year goal

✍ **WAYS TO *IMPROVE* YOUR COMPETENCE:**

✍ **WAYS TO *PROVE* YOUR COMPETENCE:**

Summary Of Chapter 6
TELL ME AGAIN WHO YOU ARE

This chapter examines several aspects of your behavior patterns which are of special importance in the high performance workplace. Below, list some of the major ideas and insights you found in the Chapter.

✍ HERE ARE SOME KEY THINGS I LEARNED ABOUT BEHAVIOR PATTERNS IN THE WORKPLACE

◊

◊

◊

◊

◊

◊

◊

◊

◊

◊

CHAPTER 6 – REVIEW QUESTIONS

1. Explore four reasons why people often resist change.

2. What are four styles of reacting to change? What are the advantages and disadvantages of each?

3. What do you mean by 'dependable'? Give examples and explain your answer.

4. Compare the roles of dependability in a traditional and a high-performance workplace.

5. Why do people take responsibility? Apply that to the high-performance workplace.

6. What assumptions about responsibility are made by credit card companies? Compare that to the assumptions made by a Theory X manager.

7. Compare the 'true cost' of dishonesty in a traditional versus a high-performance workplace. Use examples.

8. Compare the assumptions made about honesty in a traditional and a high-performance workplace.

9. Compare and contrast internal and external motivation: their similarities, differences, and roles in the traditional and high-performance workplace.

10. Explore Maslow's hierarchy of needs: what it is, how it works, and what it implies for the workplace.

11. Explore how each competency in this chapter relates to any other competency studied in this book.

CHAPTER 7

IT'S ALL IN YOUR MIND — SOMEWHERE!

Mindful Worker Competencies
Explored in Chapter 7

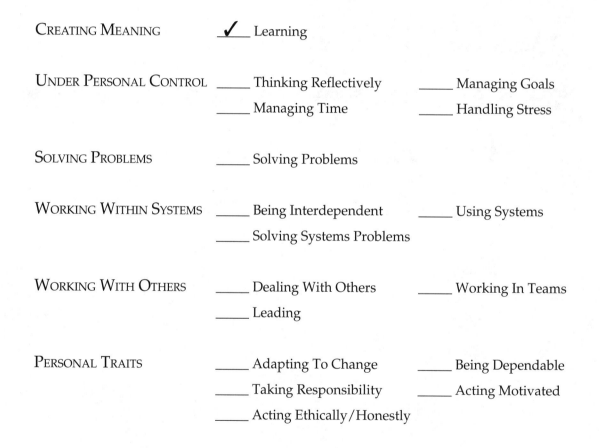

CREATING MEANING   ✓ Learning

UNDER PERSONAL CONTROL   _____ Thinking Reflectively   _____ Managing Goals

            _____ Managing Time   _____ Handling Stress

SOLVING PROBLEMS   _____ Solving Problems

WORKING WITHIN SYSTEMS   _____ Being Interdependent   _____ Using Systems

            _____ Solving Systems Problems

WORKING WITH OTHERS   _____ Dealing With Others   _____ Working In Teams

            _____ Leading

PERSONAL TRAITS   _____ Adapting To Change   _____ Being Dependable

            _____ Taking Responsibility   _____ Acting Motivated

            _____ Acting Ethically/Honestly

Exercise 7A
LEARNING INTO THE TWENTY-FIRST CENTURY

"I'm tired of learning! I'm going to go get a job!"

Have you ever heard anybody say something like that? We all have. This statement reflects a common belief that education exists in the classroom – and that it *stays* in the classroom when we leave. People who make statements like that truly believe (perhaps without much thought) that when they walk out the classroom door for the last time they are leaving 'learning' behind along with their notes, desks, and exam papers.

Is it true? In a broad sense, it never was true – and never can be true. Think of all the things we learn outside of school – and often after we've left formal education. We learn to be parents, to be husband or wife, to perform certain job tasks, to cook, to repair things, to play cards, to open and use checking accounts, to 'beat the system,' to buy or rent houses, and so forth. "Learning" follows us far beyond the classroom.

But that's not really what the person quoted really means, is it? That person is talking about leaving the formal education system. That person wants to walk away from structured group learning, where there are students and teachers, certain material to cover, and the like. Perhaps we really *can* walk away from that situation and just concentrate on our jobs.

Or can we? Some of our parents could do that, but do we really have that option any more *if* we want a satisfying job? Let's explore our options.

Let's first identify jobs which do and do not require further formal learning. For our purposes, we will define "formal learning" as situations where there is a group of learners, a designated instructor, and a structured body of material to cover. With that definition, complete the two boxes on this and the next page.

✐ LIST SOME JOBS THAT REQUIRE CONTINUED FORMAL LEARNING

✍ List Some Jobs That Do *Not* Require Continued Formal Learning

Did you have some difficulty in coming up with a lot of jobs that did *not* require continued formal learning? Part of your problem might have been that you were not sure what many jobs *did* require. Does a typist have to continue formal learning? How about a taxi driver? A fast-food burger cook?

Chances are that you put jobs in the second category that really belonged in the first one. One reality of our working world is that *most* workers have a periodic need for continued formal learning. As but one example, *every worker* in many production plants must participate in formal safety training, environmental training, and other sorts of training – even if their equipment, procedures, and paperwork are not changing. Thus all of them will undertake continued formal learning.

Even if you're right about the jobs you put in the box above, let's compare the *kinds* of jobs you listed in both boxes. Try answering the following questions.

✍ All Jobs Are Not Created Equal

Question 1   What are the characteristics of the kinds of jobs which do not require continued formal learning?

Question 2   What are the characteristic of the kinds of jobs which do require continued formal learning?

Question 3   Which group of jobs require a college education?

Question 4   Which group of jobs would you prefer to have for the rest of your life?

Probably your answers to the questions on the previous page led you to decide that the kinds of jobs you plan to have require continued learning. If you haven't already, you'll discover that continued learning is very much a characteristic of the mindful worker. You won't be leaving the classroom behind you when you leave college. You'll just be seeing it less frequently, and on a different basis.

It may not, in fact, matter as much as you think. You may discover that people's experiences, comments, and gripes are fairly much the same whether they're talking about school or work.

Let's see if that's true. Below are some common phrases; we've all heard them. Read them, and then decide what world they fit into: the job world, the school world, or both. Put a check in one blank after each phrase.

✍ Now Just Where Did I Hear That?

		Job?	Class?	Both?
1.	"If you're late again, you've had it!"	____	____	____
2.	"I'm not going to tell you again!"	____	____	____
3.	"Solve it yourself."	____	____	____
4.	"What am I supposed to do now?"	____	____	____
5.	"She's a slave-driver!"	____	____	____
6.	"Time's up. Let's go."	____	____	____
7.	"I don't know how to do that."	____	____	____
8.	"I'm so tired of this same old grind."	____	____	____
9.	"Could you say that again?"	____	____	____
10.	"They act like I don't have any brains!"	____	____	____
11.	"That's not the way we did it last week!"	____	____	____

How did you do? Probably you discovered that almost all, or all, of these phrases arise in both the work world and the school world. Do you also hear them at home, among friends, and in other situations? Interesting . . .

Exercise 7B
BEYOND MRS. HACKABERRY: LEARNING ABOUT LEARNING

Learning is one of the most constant of human activities. Babies learn to walk, talk, run, read, and so forth. Student time is focused almost exclusively on learning – and on applying what is learned. Drivers learn which intersections to avoid, when to drive at the speed limit, and how to spot a dangerous driver. Workers, and especially those planning to thrive in the 21st century, make learning a priority job task. Parents must learn a bewildering amount about how to raise children. The aged must learn how to get about with bodies that work less well than they did. Continuous learning is a human condition.

That being the case, we should all be experts on learning. Since we do it so *often*, we could naturally be expected to know how to do it *well*. We should know all about how learning works and about what to do to learn efficiently and well.

Has this happened? Not at all. Few of us learn efficiently and well. And fewer of us know much of anything about *how* we learn. We have ignored one of our most basic human traits and resources: the process of learning.

In fact, the situation is worse than that. **Most of us have incorrect ideas about how learning works**. The ways we try to learn things on the job, in school, and in our personal life are often based on misconceptions about learning. As a result, we learn poorly, spend too much time at it, and remember most things only for a short period of time.

The cartoon below summarizes one idea of how learning occurs: the relative role of teacher, student, and information.

WINTHROP   **By Dick Cavalli**

WINTHROP reprinted by permission of NEA, Inc.

Recall your school dynamics: the location of desks and chairs, who says what, the written and unwritten groundrules for conducting courses, and so forth. Then answer this question.

✍ HOW CONSISTENT WITH YOUR EXPERIENCE ARE MRS. HACKABERRY'S IDEAS?

Let's assume for a few moments that Mrs. Hackaberry has a correct perspective on how people learn. Let's assume that the dynamics of learning are basically that the teacher 'pours knowledge' into students' heads. With that perspective, try to answer the following questions.

✐ **If Mrs. Hackaberry Is Correct:**

1. What is the teacher's role in the educational process?

2. What is the student's role in the educational process?

3. Who is responsible for 'learning' in the educational process?

4. How do you explain the differences in learning success among students?

5. Why should people have to study?

6. How do you explain the fact of 'forgetting'?

7. What could someone do to improve their learning?

In fact, the 'Hackaberry Theory of Learning' is based on some very flawed assumptions about the whole learning process. Consider the following false Hackaberry assumptions and compare them to the real situation about how learning works.

False Hackaberry Assumptions About Learning	⇨	Actual Facts About Learning Dynamics
1. Learners are mentally passive.	⇨	Learners are **constantly active** in the process of learning anything.
2. Knowledge is passed on unchanged from teacher or book to learner.	⇨	Knowledge is **always changed** when moving from teacher or book to the learner.
3. Knowledge is learned in isolation, one piece at a time.	⇨	Knowledge is **always related** to other knowledge when it is learned.
4. All learners learn the same lesson in a class.	⇨	Every learner gets a **different lesson** in a class; each interprets and understands it differently.
5. The teacher is the key to learning.	⇨	The **learner** is the key to learning.

The reality is thus far different than the dynamics which Mrs. Hackaberry assumes. It's now your turn to set Mrs. Hackaberry straight. Tell her the way it *really* is by completing the following.

✍ How Do You Define 'Learning'?

What Is The Relationship Between Teacher, Student, And Knowledge?

Exercise 7C
INFORMATION PROCESSING: THE 'HOW' OF LEARNING

Do you remember in an earlier exercise that you listed some jobs that did not require continued formal learning? Write down one of those jobs on a sheet of paper. How about the assumptions underlying the Hackaberry Theory of Learning? List one of them on that sheet of paper. How about the key success competencies? List any two of them. Finally, how many employees were laid off from Fortune 500 companies in 1991.

How did you do on these questions? You probably didn't get them all. You may have had trouble with most of them. The question is: why? What made some easier to recall (or approximate) while others didn't seem to be in your mind at all any more? You *read* the answers to all of them. They may have been verbalized in class. See if you can get to the bottom of this problem.

✍ **WHY CAN'T WE REMEMBER EVERYTHING EQUALLY WELL?**

You probably identified a number of different things that affect your ability to remember something: time, the perceived importance of what you're learning, emotions, things you were thinking at the time, and so forth. All of them, however, revolve around a single dynamic process: **information processing.**

Information processing is the key to learning. It refers to the processes we go through when we pull information out of our environment, stick it in our minds, and (maybe) get it out again later when we need to use it. Let's review the fact and nature of information processing in several different ways, as follows:

1. **Information processing defined** – a model of learning in which the type and degree of information retained in the mind is directly influenced by the type and degree of cognitive processing of that information.

2. **Information processing described** – the actions we take to select information and then to do things in our minds so that we can remember and recall the information when needed later.

3. **Information processing analyzed** – consists of three basic stages:
   ◊ **Input** (to select and 'decide to learn' something)
   ◊ **Processing** (to do things with the selected information in your mind)
   ◊ **Output** (to recall it later and do something with it)

4. **Information processing abbreviated** – often abbreviated as IP (information processing) or IPO (input – processing – output).

---

5. **The information processing stages are written:** Write out each of the stages:

◊ **I** stands for _____

◊ **P** stands for _____

◊ **O** stands for _____

6. **Information processing as an image:** Imagine a cartoon character:
   ◊ Words **going in** one ear,
   ◊ Words **swirling around** inside the head, and
   ◊ Phrases **coming out** the mouth.

7. **Information processing comparison**: Compare IPO to candy production:
   ◊ Input – putting sugar and other ingredients in a machine.
   ◊ Processing – heating, cooking, and mixing ingredients.
   ◊ Output – getting M&M's out the other end of the line.

These are seven different ways to think of the same general idea of information processing. They all mean that we process information in three interactive stages.

THE INFORMATION PROCESSING CYCLE

Stage 1	INPUT	selecting and taking in information
Stage 2	PROCESSING	picturing, analyzing, defining, applying.
Stage 3	OUTPUT	bringing the information out for some use.

What does this cycle mean for us? For one thing, it helps to explain why we remember things. It also helps to explain why we forget things.

Let's take phone numbers as an example. Many of us have trouble remembering phone numbers. We look them up, but we can never remember them the next time. What's happened? Basically there's some type of **error in our Input.** The number never quite gets embedded into our minds so, we can never get it out again.

Or what about certain words that we get confused: inductive versus deductive reasoning, stalactite versus stalagmite, starboard versus port, or convex versus concave. These terms got into our minds, since we can recall them. But somehow we keep getting them mixed up. **Processing is the problem** here.

✍ **SEE IF YOU CAN LIST SOME WORDS WHOSE MEANING YOU OFTEN GET MIXED UP**

And when we are *sure* that we know something but just can't remember it right now? "On the tip of my tongue" is **an Output problem**. It's gone in. It's there. But I just can't get my hands on it right now.

Following are some situations and comments. For each one, identify whether you think it is an Input problem, a Processing problem, or an Output problem. Put the appropriate letter in front of the item. You might think that some of them could be more than one type of problem. In that case, put the letter for the most likely candidate.

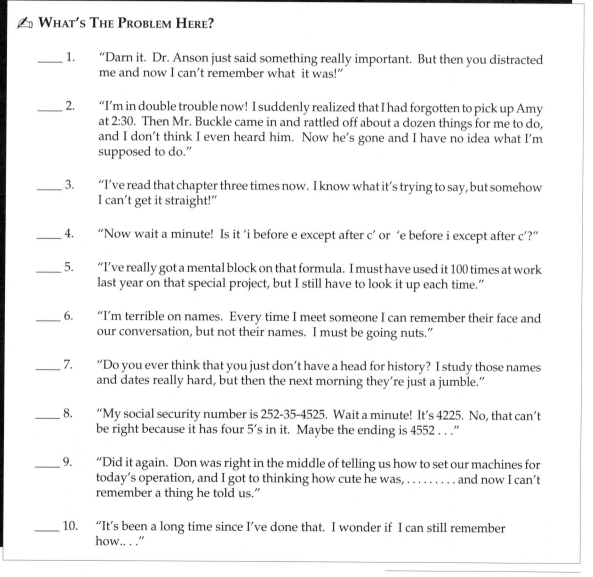

✐ WHAT'S THE PROBLEM HERE?

_____ 1. "Darn it. Dr. Anson just said something really important. But then you distracted me and now I can't remember what it was!"

_____ 2. "I'm in double trouble now! I suddenly realized that I had forgotten to pick up Amy at 2:30. Then Mr. Buckle came in and rattled off about a dozen things for me to do, and I don't think I even heard him. Now he's gone and I have no idea what I'm supposed to do."

_____ 3. "I've read that chapter three times now. I know what it's trying to say, but somehow I can't get it straight!"

_____ 4. "Now wait a minute! Is it 'i before e except after c' or 'e before i except after c'?"

_____ 5. "I've really got a mental block on that formula. I must have used it 100 times at work last year on that special project, but I still have to look it up each time."

_____ 6. "I'm terrible on names. Every time I meet someone I can remember their face and our conversation, but not their names. I must be going nuts."

_____ 7. "Do you ever think that you just don't have a head for history? I study those names and dates really hard, but then the next morning they're just a jumble."

_____ 8. "My social security number is 252-35-4525. Wait a minute! It's 4225. No, that can't be right because it has four 5's in it. Maybe the ending is 4552 . . ."

_____ 9. "Did it again. Don was right in the middle of telling us how to set our machines for today's operation, and I got to thinking how cute he was, ... and now I can't remember a thing he told us."

_____ 10. "It's been a long time since I've done that. I wonder if I can still remember how.. . ."

There is another piece of the information processing puzzle, and that is human memory. Information processing 'works' the way it does primarily because human memory works the way it does. There's a basic set of three levels of memory (it seems like many things come in sets of three). These levels differ in terms of how they work, what they do, and how long they last. It's also important to realize that the three levels feed into each other. Here's how the set works.

SENSORY MEMORY – "gets our attention"

Designed to spot something of possible interest; to pull it out from all the other things we sense at the moment.

Triggered by hearing, sight, sound, feel.

Lasts 0.1-3.0 seconds (quick as a wink)

The beginning of the Input stage

LEADS TO . . .

SHORT-TERM MEMORY – "inspects the catch"

Designed to help decide whether something is worth remembering, inspecting its nature, etc.

Follows-up after sensory memory is triggered

Lasts 30 seconds; can deal with 7-8 items at a time

Moving from Input to Processing stage

LEADS TO . . .

LONG-TERM MEMORY – "stores the catch away"

Designed to 'permanently' store the item in memory so that it can be recalled and used later.

Follows up after short-term memory says 'okay'

Lasts from minutes to a lifetime

Involved in Processing and Output stages

An analogy might help you grasp these three levels of memory and how they work together. Imagine that you've just entered a videotape rental store with a list of five videos to find. You've gone to the long back wall where those videos are liable to be – along with hundreds of others, all displayed on wall racks. The lights go out, but luckily you've got a flashlight.

Now imagine your flashlight beam playing quickly up and down and around across dozens of videos. Suddenly your beam stops – maybe that's one of the ones you want! Nope, so on goes the beam. Again it stops . . . retraces its path . . . stops fully on a video. Yep, that's one of them. You grab it, tuck it in your pocket, and on goes the flashlight beam again, looking for the next one.

Can you imagine that experience? Well, that wall of videos is our life experience: all the words, smells, pictures, and sounds that flood our every moment. The moving flashlight beam? Our awareness. As our sensory memory triggers, we sense that we've just encountered something significant. We stop and inspect it briefly, as our short-term memory kicks in. When we've decided whether or not it's significant enough (e.g., whether it's on our video order list), we do one of two things. Forget it and keep going, or take it. If we take it, that's like our choosing to process it into our long-term memory.

Let's put these two ingredients – information processing and human memory – together with the third ingredient: the methods we use in each stage. We get:

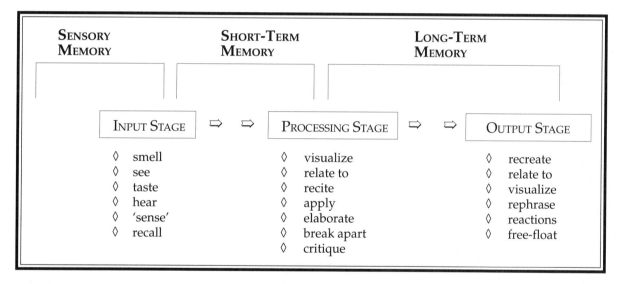

THE PROCESSES OF LEARNING

This chart puts together the three key pieces of the learning processes. Holding center stage are the three stages of information processing: **input** leads to **processing**, which leads to **output**. Notice that the three types of memory overlap information processing. Sensory memory lasts part-way through input (until you've decided it's worth noticing). Short-term memory bridges input and processing (to get the embedding activities started). Then long-term memory kicks in as you complete processing and later recall the information.

How about those diamonds beneath the three information processing stages? They are examples of some of the physical methods we use as we input, process, and output information. We'll cover them in more detail in later exercises.

Exercise 7D
INPUT: THE FIRST STAGE OF LEARNING

We overlook how many sensations deluge us each moment. A publicized method of 'breaking' spies in order to make them talk involved placing them in a situation where they had no sensations at all: nothing to hear, see, feel, or taste. Such conditions were so unnatural that the victims quickly became eager to tell their secrets just so they could 're-enter the world.'

Can you estimate how many different sounds you've heard in the last hour? Probably dozens. How about words? Can you estimate how many words you have read thus far in this chapter? Assuming you read them all, your answer is about 4,128. Taste? Feel? The same variety of sensations flood about us.

Which brings us to the process of Input. Remember where the input stage fits into the overall information processing scheme:

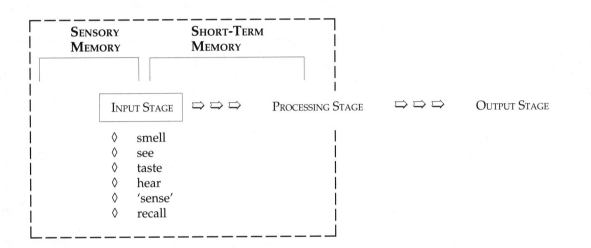

The heart of the input stage is to ignore almost all of the sensations around us but to somehow notice the important ones. For example, you just read the sentence before this one, but you ignored almost all of the words in it. You read the first paragraph on this page just a few moments ago. Try this:

HOW MANY WORDS DID YOU REALLY SEE IN THE FIRST PARAGRAPH OF THIS PAGE?

What happened to the words like 'of,' 'the,' and 'to'? You dropped them out as you read. Your **mind** automatically screened them out as not important.

The flashlight beam of your attention didn't even hesitate when it ran across those types of words. They didn't even make the first stage of information processing.

The role of the input stage is thus to sort out what's relevant from what's not relevant in your environment. If you select an item to pay attention to, it *might* eventually be something you learn and remember. If you don't select it, then you can't learn it (unless you encounter it again some other time).

Many mechanical devices are excellent at input. When programmed to react in some way to certain events, machines count, warn, track, and so forth. Unfortunately this works only when things (or people) can be prepared to react to very exact events, or very particular purposes. In our confusing real world, it's hard to know what is relevant until it occurs. We have to constantly be ready to notice and respond to many types of relevant things, often unexpected.

INFLUENCES ON INPUT

All of us have had the experience of passing by an area dozens of times, and then one time we suddenly notice a building we had never 'seen' before. It had been there all the time, our eyes had moved across it, and yet we never noticed it. But we noticed the building right next to it the very first time we passed by! Or, perhaps, we have had the experience of passing by a familiar building, and suddenly our eyes zoom in on a tiny sign in the window – the only thing new about the building.

Input is thus a tricky thing. Sometimes we react, and sometimes we don't. This seems particularly true when paying attention to something we might want to learn. What affects when and if we react to something we might want to learn? Here are some factors.

Read them, and then see how many others you can identify.

1. **Background knowledge**. If we have a lot of background knowledge in an area, it is easier to listen for what is relevant – and screen out what's not.

2. **The stakes.** If a situation is important (e.g., reviewing for the final exam or listening to a supervisor's final instructions on something), we will tend to be more active in scanning information for possible relevance.

3. **Habit.** Often we are driven by our habits – we routinely and instinctively listen or don't listen depending on the situation, the topic, etc.

4. **Our expectations**. Often we listen or read only for what we expect. If we expect something to be boring, we will absorb little. If we expect it to be relevant, then we are usually right; we take in a lot.

5. **Our mood**. Why do we 'get' less out of afternoon classes, or when we are upset? We are paying less attention, and we extract less from the stream of words and ideas around us.

✍ **LIST AT LEAST 2 OTHER INFLUENCES ON INPUT**

6.

7.

Below are a set of situations. In each case someone either failed to take in, or was very careful to take in, information which would have been useful. In the blanks before each situation write the number of the possible reason (from the list on the previous page) why they missed, or were careful to get, the important information.

✍ _____ 1. A man has moved to a new house. After work one day the next week, he worries all the way home about an important sale which he lost. When he arrives home, he realizes that he is parked in front of his old house.

_____ 2. An 11-year old boy thinks of a good idea for solving a problem that some adults are discussing. He tells them his idea but they don't pay him any attention.

_____ 3. A worker in a struggling company is sitting in the cafeteria when the plant manager and personnel officer walk by. They are discussing the possible cutbacks which may be needed if business doesn't pick up. Later the worker finds that she can repeat their whole conversation almost word-for-word.

_____ 4. Three students are listening to a special biology seminar by a famous scientist. The scientist makes a mistake in the information he presents. After the seminar two of the students – senior biology majors – start discussing the error. The third student – a student taking his first biology course – doesn't even recall the scientist making the statement.

_____ 5. A teacher introduces a new topic by saying, "This theory of advertising effectiveness has three basic parts. We'll look at them one at a time, and then we'll . . . " Later on it turns out that two-thirds of the students in the class were able to identify that the theory had three parts.

_____ 6. George gets up early to go to the library and prepare for a test. At lunch Judy comes up to him and says, "I was behind you on the way to school and honked my horn several times. You never even noticed! Are you deaf?"

_____ 7. Denise and Ellen both run plastic molding machines on different shifts in the same plant. Denise is an experienced operator and Ellen is new. On the early shift Denise's machine starts making a low growling sound. Denise immediately stops the machine and calls for a maintenance person. On the later shift Ellen's machine also starts making a low growling sound. Ellen does not stop the machine, and it burns up.

_____ 8. In the morning Joe attends the final preliminary lesson of his skydiving course. After listening and observing his instructor, he packs his parachute. When he jumps from the plane, it works. At dinner he pulls out a new recipe and prepares the dish. He leaves out one major ingredient and doubles another one. The meal really bombs!

Exercise 7E
PROCESSING: THE CRITICAL STAGE IN LEARNING

The real fun begins once we've paid attention to something. After the flashlight beam settles on a fact, an idea, something physical, etc., we decide whether or not to 'learn' it. If it fails to pass scrutiny, it's history! But if we *do* choose to learn it, then we have to *do something* with it. We must process the information into our permanent memory. Remember where the processing stage fits into the overall information processing scheme:

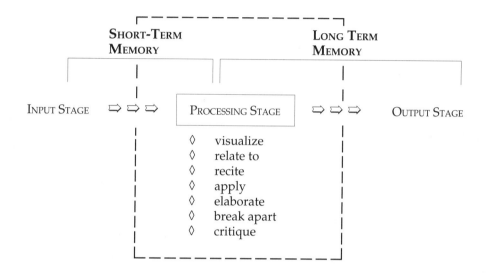

The purpose of the processing stage is to embed whatever your mind has chosen to learn deep into your long-term memory. Let's see how it works, very generally.

HOW PROCESSING WORKS

As you might guess, figuring out how our minds process information is an incredibly complicated search. Researchers are just now getting some glimpses of how the thing probably works, but much is yet unknown. To make it more difficult, much which we do seem to know is very complicated: far more complex than we have time or space for. For example, do we *really* have time for things like synapses, neural networks, and dendrites? Probably not, so here's the simplified version (some people might say it is *over*-simplified).

After you select some bit of knowledge for learning, your mind shifts it to short-term memory: sort of as a way to bring it into the production area. Your mind then reaches out into your long-term memory and selects various information, ideas, images, etc., which it thinks might relate to this new learning. It brings them into the laboratory. Then your mind processes the new information with the old: mixes, matches, molds, shapes, plays, and otherwise does things with this batch of knowledge. The result? Some new piece of long-term learning that is then re-filed with all the others – in a way that is *related* to all the others.

We might diagram that set of activities like this:

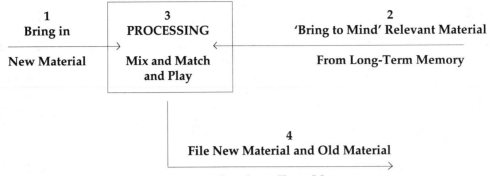

The real key to understanding all of this is to accept one reality: **we never learn one piece of knowledge without relating it to other things we know.** It is impossible to learn something in any sort of meaningful way without tying it to other things we know. Let's try it out and see if it is true.

◊ Suppose you read this: "A major oil company has introduced Milletron, a fuel additive which increases fuel economy by 45%."

◊ That information only makes sense if you 'bring to mind' all sorts of other information, such as these:

- What a 'major oil company' is. (also, what 'oil' is, what a 'company' is, etc.).

- What each word means: what is 'introduced'? What does it mean in this context (surely not giving each other your names)?

- What is fuel, and that it implies automobile fuel (rather than toast, which is another kind of fuel).

- What an 'additive' is, and what you do with it (including mental images of pouring a can of liquid into your gas tank).

- What 45% means, and that it is a high percentage. Also, that high percentages are good in this case (as opposed to something that increases gas pollution by 45%).

- Things to be suspicious of, such as possible side effects (rots the engine, pollutes the atmosphere), or costs ($7.50 a bottle).

And so forth. If you had time to do it, you would discover that just trying to make sense of that one sentence requires that you recall, sort through, and apply hundreds, if not thousands, of pieces of information which you already have.

The message is hopefully clear. Any time you choose to learn something new, you call up many items you already know in order to 'make sense' out of that new information. You put it into long-term memory mainly by linking it strongly to other things that are already in your memory.

Below are four startling pieces of information. Your mind tells you that you want to remember them. You need to process them with existing information. Pick one and follow the instructions.

✍ **List Ten Items Of Information You Can 'Bring To Mind' To Help You Process The Following Announcements:**

- The Food and Drug Administration has approved a new chemical which will eliminate cholesterol in all beef products.

- Starting this term, all students with an A average will no longer have to take the final exam.

- The IRS has decreased income taxes by 10% for all of those filing their returns electronically.

- A fast-food chain has added a 10% surcharge for drive-through orders.

Is It Possible To Think Of Anything You Can Learn Without Bringing To Mind Existing Information?

In fact, you can 'hear yourself think' while you are bringing to mind information out of your long-term memory. Consider the phrases listed below. Doesn't each one of them really let you know that you are tapping your long-term memory? For example, what if something you hear or read causes you to say (out loud or to yourself), "That reminds me of . . . "? What are you doing? You are bringing into your conscious mind the memory of whatever it reminds you of. Look at these 'brings to mind' phrases, and then try to **add at least two other phrases**.

✍ **Some Natural 'Brings To Mind' Phrases**

"That reminds me of . . . "

"Now I see . . . "

"That doesn't fit with . . . "

"Couldn't you do that another way . . . "

"That explains something that's been bothering me . . . "

"Could I use that idea in order to . . . "

◊

◊

Some Groundrules For Processing

After we bring our new information together with selected information from our long-term memory, we process them together. There are many different ways to do this, and everyone has preferred methods. However, some groundrules will help you as you seek to process new knowledge more effectively. Here are three key groundrules:

◊ THE MORE PROCESSING, THE BETTER THE LEARNING

Each time you process a piece of information, it leaves a trace in your mind. If you process it once, you have one trace. Twice? Deeper traces, etc. Does this help to explain why repeating things sometimes helps you learn?

◊ THE MORE VARIED THE PROCESSING, THE BETTER THE LEARNING

Repeating something several times leaves a deep trace in one place. If your mind happens to wander by that spot, you will easily notice the deep trace. But isn't it better to leave several traces in *different* places? That way your mind is more likely to wander close by. So if you repeat something, write it down, picture it, and relate it to something, you have left traces all over the place. Far much better likelihood that you will be able to remember and use the information later.

◊ THE MORE ENERGETIC THE PROCESSING, THE BETTER THE LEARNING

Ever try to study something when your mind was far away, you were disinterested in the subject, or you were just going through the motions? Didn't work very well, did it? At best you left a lightly-scratched trace, easy for your mind to overlook as it hunted for the information. Compare that to things you learned at a really scary or excited moment. Bang! Instant learning!

Examining Some Of Our Specific Learning Processes

There are many mental processes we use naturally when learning new material. Here are some common ones. As you read about them, scan your own experiences and notice how often you also use them as you make sense out of new material.

Visualize

Most of us make mental pictures when we are learning new things. We have a picture in our minds as we read a passage, listen to song lyrics, hear a description of a person we have not met, or try to understand a process someone is telling us about. Try to give or receive directions to someone's house without visualizing the route! Listen to someone relate a conversation, and you will be picturing it with them.

Question

Our active minds are continually asking questions as we learn. What does this mean? Where does it fit? Does it conflict with other things I know? Is it true? If it's true, how can I use it? Did I misunderstand? You can use the ability to ask questions as a very powerful means of learning. Interestingly, sometimes we can't remember something directly but we **can** remember the questions we asked ourselves as we were trying to remember it. And we can then use *this* awareness as the clue we need to recall the information itself.

COMPARE TO

As you hear a new piece of information about something, it is natural to compare it to what you already know about that subject. Does it fit with what you know? Does it extend what you know? Does it conflict with what you think you know? Suppose you read this statement: "Memorizing is the only useful way to learn." Watch your mind comparing that statement to what you've just been learning, to your own past experience, and so forth. Often we learn by comparing new with old.

BREAK APART

Let's suppose you were shopping for a new car and received a brochure filled with information on the Argus-C. Your mind couldn't deal with all of it at once, so you'd break it into pieces and deal with one at a time: cost, looks, features, mileage, and so forth. To learn a procedure, we break it into stages.

ELABORATE

What do we mean by 'elaborate'? We take a new item and add things. If you encounter the phrase 'learn by practicing' you might elaborate it by adding various other things you know. It might go back into your long-term memory looking something like this: "Learn by practicing in various ways and at various times, spread over a considerable period of time, with frequent feedback." Adding things to new information is a powerful way to learn and remember it.

APPLY

A very important way to process information is to apply it to things. Explore this idea of processing information. See if it applies to learning a new technique on the assembly line. How about when you watch someone move on the athletic field? Does it fit with how you learn new recipes, or song lyrics, or a dance step? You will discover that the mere act of trying to apply new knowledge helps you to learn it. Why? Because you have to be sure you understand it. And you relate it to things you know.

✍ **ADD AT LEAST TWO OTHER PROCESSES TO THIS LIST**
    (Hint: Ask yourself what you've done to learn this stuff.)

INTRODUCING TWO REVOLUTIONARY NEW ENTERTAINMENT SYSTEMS

Let's bring this segment on processing information into long-term memory to a close by examining two events. An international company is introducing a revolutionary entertainment system: one we'll all want to buy. It is introducing it on June 25 in the country of Burgoostan, and on June 26 in the United States of America. Read below about both announcements, and watch your minds seek to learn about this new entertainment system.

Announcement of the System In Burgoostan: June 25

"This revolutionary system consists of a thin cor-like strip shaped like lubchucks, but somewhat more burgly. They are scrimmed into a machine about the size of an elburget, and they have a bittel capability. They are frump-powered. They can perform all of the functions of sartoris, kannel, treemonts, and pteractine. The machine costs about 932 kurush and the strips about 27 corona each."

STOP RIGHT HERE! What was your mind trying to do?

✎ _____

_____

_____

Now read the next day's announcement, and again watch your mind work on this extraordinary new entertainment system.

Announcement of the System in the United States: June 26

"This revolutionary system consists of a thin plastic-like strip shaped like a bandaid, except smaller. They are fed into a machine about the size of a cigarette pack, and they have a projection capability. They are solar-powered. They can perform all the functions of CD players, videorecorders, computer disks, and cellular phones. The machine costs about $1,250 and the strips about $59 each."

Did you watch your mind at work? You were busy getting a mental image of something about like a bandaid, a cigarette pack, etc. Analyzing the capabilities of CDs and computers and such. Thinking about what $1,250 meant (and, perhaps, where you could get that kind of money). Breaking the information into sections. And so forth.

You were, in short, taking in this new package of information, recalling what you knew that fit the situation, and processing the two sets of data together. Then you were filing it back into long-term memory again. You were processing.

Exercise 7F
OUTPUT: THE PAYOFF IN LEARNING

All of the input and processing have one payoff: recalling something from your mind so that you can use it in some fashion. Remember where the output stage fits into the overall information processing scheme:

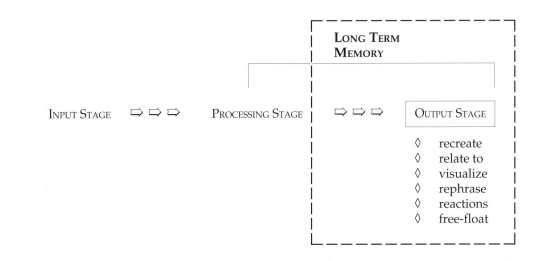

PURPOSE

The purpose of the output stage is, of course, to get knowledge *out* of storage in your long-term memory. Where does it go? Into what's called your working memory – the production facilities of your mind. When you 'bring something to mind' you are bringing it into the active, conscious area of thought so that you can *do* something with it.

Sometimes we bring it up in order to do physical things: solve math problems, write essays, answer multiple choice questions, fill out forms, etc. Often, though, we do something odd. We bring things into our working memory so that we can use them purely in our minds. Does that sound weird? Well, spend a couple of minutes planning the rest of your day. Recall the name of your favorite (or least favorite) teacher last year. Do you have enough gas to get home? Have you forgotten to do something today? How much money is in your wallet? Where do you go after this class? What's the last argument you had?

Every time you asked yourself one of those questions, you dove into your long-term memory to drag out information. You used it only in your head – no one looking at you would have had any idea what you were thinking. Output, then, can be for physical purposes or for mental purposes.

How do we pull the right information out of all the facts and experiences that are stored in our memories? Unfortunately, that question doesn't have a tidy answer. We do it in different ways depending on our personality, the situation, the timing, how deeply it is buried, and all sorts of other factors. We have as many ways to extract (output) information as we do to process it in the first place. Here, however, are some proven methods that people find useful.

USEFUL STRATEGIES FOR RECALLING INFORMATION

RECREATE THE SITUATION

As we learn something, we naturally relate it to what's happening about us: sounds, noise, people, other events. To recall that learning, we can try to recall that moment in time. Who was doing what? How did it look or feel? What sounds were there? What were you thinking at the time? By bringing back the moment (or only a piece of it), we can often bring back the learning. Or if someone said that they loved green cars – "... like that new Ford color," we could recall the moment we saw such a car and can then dredge up the color they mean.

RELATE TO

As we learned earlier, when we process information we **always** relate it to other things we know, which we have pulled up from long-term memory. An important trick in recalling knowledge is simply to recall not the knowledge we are seeking but rather the other knowledge it is related to. For example, you learn the concept of electron flow by relating it to water flowing in a pipe. When you need to recall the concept, you might first think of water pipes, which leads you to electron flow.

VISUALIZE

A favorite technique for recalling something is to use mental pictures. How often have you remembered a fact or idea by first getting a picture of what the page of text looked like, or your page of notes? How about visualizing where the instructor was sitting when she made the point? How about learning a procedure by getting a step-by-step picture of it in your head as the instructor goes over it, and *then* remembering that picture as you try to recall the procedure?

REPHRASE

A favorite student complaint is, "You said it different in class than you did on the test." That kind of complaint doesn't impress teachers, and is less likely to impress employers. Try instead to recall something by rephrasing it. If it's in words, jot it down in pictures. If in numbers, try words. If asked, "What is Maslow's hierarchy of needs?" rephrase it as, "What do people want to protect the most?"

RECALL YOUR REACTIONS

Remember that one of the groundrules for processing related to the *intensity* of your mental actions? Use that reality when recalling things. What if it's late and the teacher starts a new topic? Your reaction might be, "Oh, no. Give me a break!" Guess what? You can deliberately recall that reaction, and the learning is liable to trail in along with it. If something is interesting, try to recall your feeling of interest. If it sounds really silly, try to recall that. And so forth.

There are many other recall methods, but these will give you the idea. Think about the ones we have discussed, and then answer the following question.

✍ How Do Our Likelihood And Methods Of Recall Relate To Our Processing?

Let's practice what we've learned about output. In Exercise 3C we introduced the key aspect of learning by using several different quick activities. Try to recall that experience and answer these questions. As you do so, get in touch with how you are searching through your memory.

✍ Recalling The Keys To Learning

◊   What does IP stand for?

◊   What does IPO stand for?

◊   How many ways did we process those points?

◊   Which of those activities can you remember?

◊   Does recalling one help recall another?

◊   Can you visualize going through that process?

◊   Can you recall what you were thinking/feeling? If so, what was it?

◊   Do you remember where you were when doing them?

◊   Are you aware of your mind answering these questions?

Exercise 7G
WHEN THE SYSTEM BREAKS DOWN: FORGETTING

Learning and remembering are imperfect events, even for skilled learners. Below is some information about remembering and forgetting. For each reality, see if you can use information processing concepts to explain what might be happening.

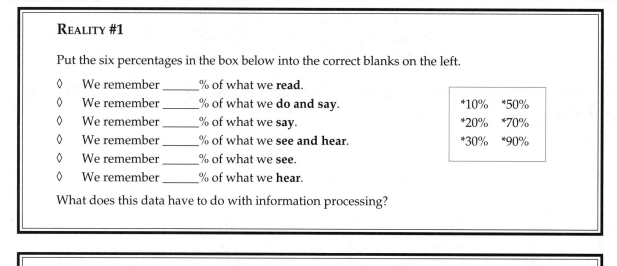

REALITY #1

Put the six percentages in the box below into the correct blanks on the left.

◊   We remember _____% of what we **read**.

◊   We remember _____% of what we **do and say**.

◊   We remember _____% of what we **say**.

◊   We remember _____% of what we **see and hear**.

◊   We remember _____% of what we **see**.

◊   We remember _____% of what we **hear**.

*10%	*50%
*20%	*70%
*30%	*90%

What does this data have to do with information processing?

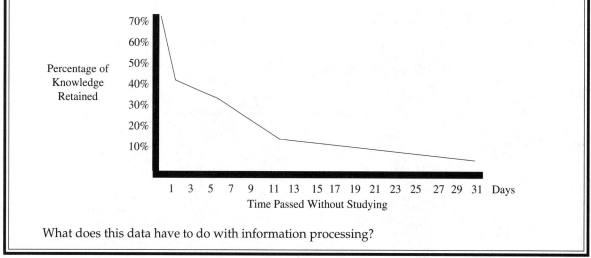

REALITY #2

Here is a chart which shows how much we typically remember, over time, about what we have learned in a course.

Percentage of Knowledge Retained

70%
60%
50%
40%
30%
20%
10%

1   3   5   7   9   11   13   15   17   19   21   23   25   27   29   31   Days

Time Passed Without Studying

What does this data have to do with information processing?

Reality #3

Here is another chart. This one shows how much learning is retained when a person studies at various times after the class.

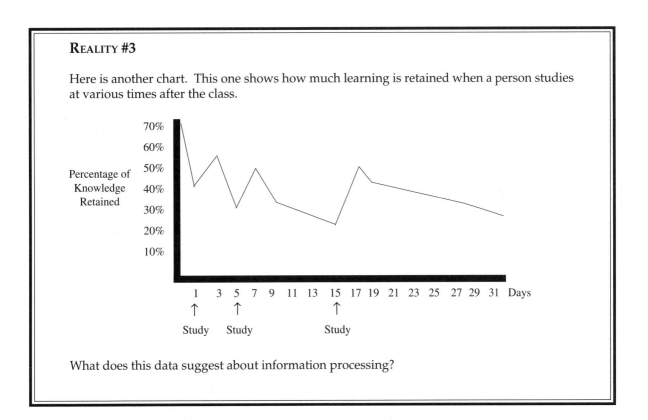

What does this data suggest about information processing?

✍ **List Some Of The Reasons Why People Forget. A Couple Of Them Are Given.**

◊   *Time lapses and the 'memory trace' grows cold.*

◊   *Our memory is only tied to one trace, which is hard to find.*

◊

◊

◊

◊

◊

Exercise 7H
WHY IS THAT MEDICINE GOOD FOR ME?

We know a lot about the methods used by good learners when studying. Only gradually, however, have we gotten a good sense of *why* some of these methods work — and why some other ones don't work as well. Mrs. Hackaberry, with her 'pour it in' theory of learning, can't explain the success of these methods. But information processing *can*.

Below are listed a set of methods for studying, and an indication of whether or not they work. Find an explanation for each method's success or failure based on information processing theory. A couple of examples are given.

✍ **EXPLAIN EACH FACTOID BASED ON INFORMATION PROCESSING THEORY**

1. Reviewing immediately after class improves learning.

   Partly because it lets us make another deep memory trace while the first ones (hearing it in class, making notes, etc.) are still hot.

2. Cramming late on the night before the test doesn't work very well.

   The fatigue factor makes our traces, and our links to related items, blurry and uncertain. Fresh minds make the sharpest memory traces.

3. Highlighting only selected material seems to promote learning.

4. Looking for clues (such as key words, sub-heads, definitions, etc.) improves learning.

5. Recopying our notes in exactly the same way we first took them does not seem to be very helpful.

---

6. Rewriting our notes with a different order and phrasing seems to help us learn.

7. Stating the key points out loud definitely improves our learning.

8. Skimming a new chapter before reading it carefully helps us learn better.

9. Writing down questions about what we're studying usually helps us learn.

10. Repeating information over seems to help short-term recall, but does not seem to help us apply the learning in different situations.

11. Self-testing our knowledge (asking ourselves what we know and don't know) tends to promote learning.

12. Practicing for a relatively short period several different times seems to lead to more learning than heavy cramming once or twice.

✒ **DISCUSS THIS QUOTE**: *"It is impossible to conceive of a passive learner."*

Exercise 7I
LEARNING ON THE JOB

Being a skilled learner – a master of information processing – obviously pays off for the college student. You're there to learn, and anything that helps you do that is of benefit.

But what about the workplace? Well, remember the mindful worker we explored in the first chapter. This is the person who is, in many ways, learning for a living, adjusting to changes in equipment, procedures, organization, purposes, and the like. Who is part of a group who continually study how to make their organization more effective, their products more reliable, their systems more efficient. Mindful workers are continual learners.

Let's close this chapter by exploring the mindful worker's world. Below are listed some typical 'student tasks.' Use your experience, your knowledge, and your creative imagination to identify times when the mindful worker would also be performing those 'learner tasks.' A couple of examples are given.

LEARNING ON AND ABOUT THE JOB

1. TAKING NOTES

    ◊ *Listening to a salesman describe a new chemical that the company might want to buy.*

    ◊ *When your boss is rattling off things to do when she's out of town.*

    ✍

    ✍

    ✍

2. READING TECHNICAL MATERIAL

    ◊ *A new corporate system for accounting for the disposal of dangerous chemicals in a printing shop.*

    ◊ *A manual for installing and operating a new fry-making machine.*

    ✍

    ✍

    ✍

3. COLLECTING AND ANALYZING DATA

    ◊ *Tracking sales of a new product to justify heavy advertising costs in a clothing store.*

    ◊ *Evaluating returned goods to determine the most common type of flaw.*

    ✍

    ✍

    ✍

4. MEMORIZING INFORMATION

    ◊   *Learning sales figures, trends, and patterns in preparation for a major report to a corporate vice-president.*

    ◊   *Learning a sales pitch for a new product before meeting a customer.*

    ✍

    ✍

    ✍

5. LISTENING TO A LECTURE

    ◊   *Listening to an engineer explain the operations of a complex new computerized sampling system in an electronics plant.*

    ◊   *Attending a two-day mandatory corporate seminar on sexual harassment in the workplace.*

    ✍

    ✍

    ✍

✍ **CAN YOU THINK OF A 'LEARNER TASK' THAT IS *NOT* IMPORTANT IN THE WORKPLACE?**

Exercise 7J
UPDATING THE FLOW OF INFORMATION PROCESSING

You began this chapter with a three-stage conception of information processing, with an overlapping set of memory types and physical/mental actions. When learning about the Processing Stage you also studied the role of prior knowledge in helping you process new information. Putting all of that together creates an updated version of information processing, as follows.

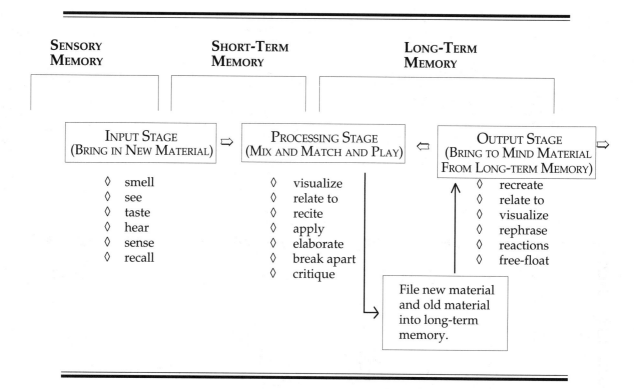

Does this updated process chart make even clearer what's happening in your mind as you learn something new? It's happening in your head even as you read these words. It's a continual process, and it's one which you can significantly control. You can learn to become a more effective learner – and mindful worker – if you understand, practice, and apply these information processing concepts.

✍ Can you write a one page explanation of the chart on this page?
Try it on a separate sheet of paper.

Exercise 7K
LEARNING: MAKING YOUR MAP

Now it's time to make your personal map of the second mindful worker competency: learning. As with the last chapter, you need to do three things. First, read and add to the description of an exceptional learner, in the box below. Then assess your own state of competence in comparison to that description, and finally set a 2-3 year goal for yourself.

✍ PROFILE OF AN EXCEPTIONAL LEARNER: Someone who can listen carefully and extract all the key information from what another person is saying. Who can smoothly process that information in a variety of ways, including relating it to things already known. Someone who can apply the new information appropriately when it is needed. Someone who can remember things for a long time.

Someone who:

Someone who:

✍ RATE YOUR OWN COMPETENCE AT LEARNING

HORRIBLE				FAIR					EXCELLENT
1	2	3	4	5	6	7	8	9	10

"X" point = current status   "Circle" point = 2-3 year goal

✍ WAYS TO *IMPROVE* YOUR COMPETENCE:

✍ WAYS TO *PROVE* YOUR COMPETENCE:

Summary Of Chapter 7
IT'S ALL IN YOUR MIND, SOMEWHERE!! LEARNING HOW WE LEARN

What did you take away from this chapter? Summarize below the key things you learned about learning. It may help you organize your thoughts to imagine yourself explaining how to learn to someone else, based on what you've gotten from this chapter.

✍ HERE ARE SOME KEY THINGS I LEARNED ABOUT LEARNING

◊

◊

◊

◊

◊

◊

◊

◊

◊

◊

◊

Chapter 7 – Review Questions

1. List and explain four facts about how learning occurs.

2. Describe the three stages of information processing: what they are, what they do, and how they relate to each other.

3. List and explain five factors which have major influence on our input.

4. Describe and explain the four activities that make up 'processing' of new information: what they are, how they work, and how they relate to each other.

5. Describe the role that 'prior knowledge' plays in our processing of new information.

6. List and explain four specific learning processes that you use especially often when processing information. Use examples.

7. Explain how the 'output' stage of information processing works.

8. How does our likelihood and methods of recall relate to our processing?

9. List and explain four reasons why people forget things.

10. Why is conscious control of your information processing an important competence for a mindful worker?

11. List several techniques or habits which help or hinder your learning. Use the dynamics of information processing to explain *why* each technique or habit helps or hinders.

CHAPTER 8

IMPROVING YOURSELF AS A MINDFUL WORKER

You have ended the past six chapters by making a map for each competency. You have rated your own performance, set goals, and identified how to prove your competence and how to improve. It is now time to pull all of this together into a long-term plan of action for your own personal improvement. To begin, review all of the mindful worker competencies we have covered. Select five of them that you most want to improve and list them below: the most important, or maybe those where you are weakest.

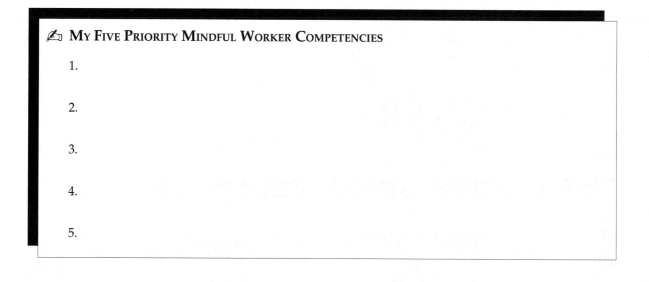

✍ **MY FIVE PRIORITY MINDFUL WORKER COMPETENCIES**

1.

2.

3.

4.

5.

You are going to create a plan of action for each of those five priority competencies by doing the following things.

STEP 1   Identify *one specific goal* related to that competency that you think you can achieve within about six months or so (you need to specify a timetable).

STEP 2   Establish *three enabling goals* which you will need to do in order to accomplish the major goal. If you don't remember enough about enabling goals, check Chapter 4!

STEP 3   Identify *how you will know* that the major goal has been met. What evidence will you find that shows that you have accomplished it?

STEP 4   Identify the *reward(s)* you will give yourself when you reach each enabling goal (small rewards) and the major goal (*major* reward!).

What will all of this accomplish? It will help you take that most difficult first step from 'book-learning' to genuine personal growth. You will take some personally-relevant aspects of what you've studied and you will make them part of your actual life and growth. If you keep going for six months, you can make it for the full 2-3 year period of your goals. Then you'll do more . . .

To make sure you understand what you'll be doing, here is a *short* example of this type of goal planning. Your plan will of course be different, but this should give you the idea. For this example we will use the mindful worker competency of 'listening' – one that we did not cover in this text.

Target Competency: Listening

1. Identify one specific goal (and time frame):

   By the end of six months I will be able to identify all (up to fifteen) key points in a day's lecture in any of my classes.

2. Identify three enabling goals:

   First, I will identify and write down all the clues which each of my instructors use to indicate that material is important: phrases, mannerisms, tone of voice, etc.

   Second, I will star each point in my notes when the instructor used one of the clues I have identified.

   Third, I will start comparing my notes (and starred items) with those of another student in the class. I will use the results to improve my techniques.

3. Identify how I will know I have met my major goal:

   After my notes are mostly consistent with those of another student (and no later than five months from now), I will show my notes from three class periods to the instructor. I will tell the instructor what I've been doing and will ask the instructor to check my work. If I've missed some key points I'll ask the instructor's help in figuring out what other clues I can look for. Then I'll practice them some more.

4. Identify my rewards for meeting each goal:

   When I reach each of my enabling goals I will treat myself to a good dinner at a nice restaurant. When I accomplish my major goal I will arrange things so that I can spend an entire weekend doing just what I want to do.

Your goals, evidence, and especially rewards would obviously differ from these. But hopefully this will give you guidance as you tackle the *final activities* in this text: *your* five priority plans.

✍ PRIORITY COMPETENCY #1:

1. Identify one specific goal (and time frame):

2. Identify three enabling goals:

3. Identify how I will know I have met my major goal:

4. Identify my rewards for meeting each goal:

✐ **Priority Competency #2:**

1. Identify one specific goal (and time frame):

2. Identify three enabling goals:

3. Identify how I will know I have met my major goal:

4. Identify my rewards for meeting each goal:

✍ Priority Competency #3:

1. Identify one specific goal (and time frame):

2. Identify three enabling goals:

3. Identify how I will know I have met my major goal:

4. Identify my rewards for meeting each goal:

✎ **PRIORITY COMPETENCY #4:**

1. Identify one specific goal (and time frame):

2. Identify three enabling goals:

3. Identify how I will know I have met my major goal:

4. Identify my rewards for meeting each goal:

✍ PRIORITY COMPETENCY #5:

1. Identify one specific goal (and time frame):

2. Identify three enabling goals:

3. Identify how I will know I have met my major goal:

4. Identify my rewards for meeting each goal:

This text has tried to accomplish several things:

1. To give you a realistic, thoughtful view of what the 'world of work' will probably be like in this decade and beyond. This view does not cover all typical work (remember the darker side of working, from Chapter 1). But it does cover the most interesting, challenging, and rewarding types of work.

2. To give you an awareness of (and some beginning skill with) the types of crucial competencies which will perhaps be the difference between your success and failure in that workplace.

3. To present to you some of the choices and decisions which you will be making in terms of how you approach and fit into the workplace of the 21st century.

4. To give you some sense of your greater and lesser strengths in terms of these competencies.

Beyond these types of objectives, however, lie two others of the greatest importance. They are listed below.

I Hope That This Experience Has Helped You To:

1. Become a thoughtful, interested explorer of all of the workplace realities and workforce competencies which we have *not* talked about (in many cases, because we are not yet aware of them).

2. See the need for, develop, and implement your own personal plan of action for becoming an ever-stronger member of the mindful workforce. It needs you.

There is a "Message to the Author" sheet on the next page of this book. I urge you to fill it in, mail it, and help me improve this book for those who use it later.

Offering suggestions is a very important role for the mindful worker seeking to improve the systems we all learn and work within . . .

Thanks and good luck,

Curtis Miles

MESSAGE TO THE AUTHOR

I've got some suggestions for how you could improve *The Mindful Worker*.
Here they are:

I suggest that you **add**:

I suggest that you **delete**:

I suggest that you **change**:

I suggest that you **correct**:

I have these **other ideas**:

(Just cut out this page, fold it, and drop it in the mail to us with your stamp.)

Re: *The Mindful Worker*
c/o H&H Publishing Company
1231 Kapp Drive
Clearwater, FL 33765